IN SEARCH OF COURAGE:
An Introvert's Story

"Steve Friedman's book, *In Search of Courage*, brings forward the struggles many introverts deal with on a day-to-day basis. Steve's story is an authentic one of self-discovery—the pains, joys and acceptance of being and embracing who you are in spite of the influence of our extroverted, highly digital society. The road to authenticity is often upstream. Steve swims it, in spite of the currents."

-Norma T. Hollis, America's Leading Authenticity Expert and author of *Ten Steps to Authenticity* and *Blueprint for Engagement: Authentic Leadership*

"Kudos to Steve Friedman for sharing such a personal journey through the challenges of being an introvert in an extroverted world. As an introvert myself, I can relate to so many situations in his captivating book. This book will help others feel less alone in their own journeys."

-Stephanie Chandler, author of *The Nonfiction Book Publishing Plan* and CEO of the Nonfiction Authors Association

"While searching for personal courage, Steve Friedman transcends individual conflicts to explore themes of self-awareness and belonging. In the tradition of Maya Angelou, Richard Rodriguez, and Paul Monette, *In Search of Courage* illuminates, through a very personal lens, universal insights bright with wisdom and heart."

-Roger Leslie, PhD, author of *From Inspiration to Publication* and Owner of Paradise Publishing House

"Wow! What a compelling life story. I enjoyed it and found myself pausing to reflect often. I love that Friedman married the emotional reality with his professional life. So often it's one or the other. As men we are socialized to hide our emotions using alcohol or other substances/behaviors. Friedman's courageous sharing of his pilgrimage will resonate with many. Congratulations on the start of an exciting journey of sharing the written word."

-Blaise Dismer, MSW author of *Homebound No More: How I Beat Agoraphobia*

"Steve Friedman shares his personal stories in such a way that we care for him while learning about ourselves. It was almost as if I could feel his pain, anxiety, and sadness as he endured each struggle. I couldn't stop reading to find out the next roadblock he faced along his journey and how he coped with it. Well done!"

-Mike Kowis, Esq., tax attorney, professor, and award-winning author

"I enjoyed reading Steve Friedman's story. His challenges and the ways in which he faced them are very relatable. Whether you're an introvert or not, you're sure to recognize yourself or those you know in these stories. The anecdotes are quite amusing as well. An insightful read."

-Kenneth Rosenberg, novelist and author of
*Memoirs of a Starving Artist: An Itinerant Writer's
Journey through an Unconventional Life*

IN SEARCH OF
COURAGE

An Introvert's Story

IN SEARCH OF
COURAGE
An Introvert's Story

Steve Friedman

Peavine Press, LLC
Houston, Texas

Publisher: Peavine Press, LLC
Houston, Texas USA

www.BeyondIntroversion.com
BeyondIntroversion@gmail.com

ISBN: 978-1-7342211-1-4
Library of Congress Catalog Number: 2019917508

NOTE: All events described in this autobiographical work
were shared through the perceptions of the author. Some
people depicted are not identified by their real name.

Cover image credit: © Bashkatov/stock.adobe.com

Thanks for reading *In Search of Courage: An Introvert's Story*.
I hope you will be captivated by my experiences
and inspired by my journey.

FREE BONUS – LOG IN FOR PHOTOS FOR EACH CHAPTER

www.BeyondIntroversion.com/In-Search-of-Courage/Photos

CONTENTS

DEDICATION

To my wife Jennifer, the light of my life, who
provides me with guidance, unending patience,
and true love. She has always believed in me, even
when I didn't have faith in myself, and has forever
encouraged me to reach for my dreams.

PROLOGUE

During a rare talk with Dad in his latter years, I realized he was not just a sweet clarinetist, but also a *phenomenal* musician, earning first chair at the University of Alabama's Million Dollar Marching Band. Music was his passion. Yet, he was overcome by pragmatism and obligation. Thus, he shelved his dreams of pursuing a musical education at Julliard and taking a stab at a career in New York City in order to fulfill his commitment to join the family business.

As a shy, reserved boy, I tended to hide behind my written words. My childhood friend and I spent one summer vacation publishing a neighborhood newsletter, *The Belle Meade News*, at the age of eleven. After writing and co-editing for my high school newspaper, *The Sword & Shield*, I dreamt of being a writer or journalist—to share my thoughts and observations through my pen.

However, practicality proved to get the better of me, and I bent to the same pressure my dad endured those many decades earlier, tabling my dreams to pursue a business profession. Throughout my career, I often avoided arguments by deliberating my positions through notes and letters. I relied upon journaling through my darkest moments to try to sort out the competing forces in my head.

Though content and proud of the family he led in his 80s, my dad lamented not chasing his vision. With this indelible memory, my dad stirred me to bring my thoughts, fears, and passions forward through the reflections and stories that follow.

During my mom's last days, she beseeched me to finish my stories and to share them with the world. This inspiration helped carry me through my years of writing and re-writing. Along the way, I've met many amazing people that have enhanced my life's journey, which began in such an auspicious way.

However, today, I tremble at the stress and strains I endured through a turbulent childhood and decades of corporate work life. I reflect on my destructive choices to cope with my earliest of insecurities and frequent temptations. Throughout the years, I struggled with many opportunities to exhibit courage and confidence. My personal journey was taxing both on me and my loved ones. Through these thoughts and sagas, I hope others may garner the bravery to overcome their own demons and challenges.

My story starts as a young boy in the suburbs of Birmingham, Alabama…

FREE BONUS – LOG IN FOR PHOTOS
FOR EACH CHAPTER

www.BeyondIntroversion.com/In-Search-of-Courage/Photos

SECTION ONE – TURBULENCE

CHAPTER 1: THE CLOSETS

My favorite time was alone time.

My mom seemed to worry about my solitude a lot more than I did. "Why don't we set up a play date with a friend?"

"I'm fine. No one I really want to hang out with, Mom."

"What about at kindergarten? Maybe get to know them better?"

"I don't know, Mommy."

"You should try, Stephen. It'd be good for you."

"Fine," I sighed, anxious to move on from the subject.

My efforts to make friends were generally gawky and unsuccessful. I always felt a bit odd, unable to talk to the other kids at school. Or maybe it was because I was the only kid in kindergarten routinely donning a suit and tie... at age six! My parents didn't force that upon me. I just felt compelled to dress up, perhaps to mimic my dad who always looked dapper when he went to work. In order to appease Mom, one day at school I clung next to Isaac Furman. He was a popular guy amongst the dozen kids my age at our Jewish kindergarten.

I gulped down the pit in my throat, bit my lower lip, and blurted: "Hey. What's up?"

Isaac took a long look at me in my suit.

"Hey, come here. Let me show you something," Isaac whispered as he pointed into a closet. As I peeked in, he suddenly shoved me into the closet and wedged a chair against its doorknob, trapping me inside. Through the crack I could hear him gathering the others. I tried to push my way out without any luck. I sensed he was pointing at me, caught behind the door. He received adulation and laughter while I fought back my anger and tears. I pushed harder. But I chose not to beat on the door or yell for help. I didn't want to give Isaac that satisfaction or make things worse for me. I was humiliated enough. Finally, I could hear the teacher enter the room and the others shuffled away from the closet.

The teacher pried the chair away and let me out. "Are you okay?"

I slinked out of the closet. Not wanting to attract any further attention, I mumbled, "I'm fine. I don't want to talk about it."

I escaped to the bathroom and hung my head. *Why did they do that to me? Why me? What's wrong with me?*

The day dragged on. Later when I got home from school, I headed straight for my clothes closet. It was the best part of my room, and of the whole house as far as I was concerned. When I opened my closet door I faced a two-foot high wall, designed to accommodate the staircase below, followed by the metal pole holding up all my hanging clothes. But when I peeled back my jeans, corduroys, and fancy clothes to the deeper right side, another higher tier was revealed. As I climbed onto the second level, I turned to face the door and used the plywood plank that lay above the clothes pole as my desktop. I loved it because it was unique, but also because it was the solitude I craved growing up. It was a little nirvana for me, often holed away in the top of my two-story bedroom closet for hours doing homework and hobbies. On this day I crawled inside to escape.

However, outside my closet, I never had a lot of friends. I was a shy kid at heart. That was me, who I was. Nevertheless, my mom continued to encourage me to make friends and have play dates like my older sister Renee. She and I played around the house as we grew up. She certainly had a calling to socialize with countless friends while I occasionally played with my only friend, Steven Schwartz, who lived up the block. We did what kids do at that age—games, TV, bikes. That's excitement to two seven-year-olds in the '70s. At eight, Steven moved to New York City. My lone pal was gone.

I then turned to my backyard neighbor, Roger. We formed a close bond playing with matchbox cars in his backyard dirt, often for hours on end. We built roads and bridges, waterways and parking lots, and drove our cars throughout our land of make-believe. I came home with my arms and hands dark brown from hours in the dirt, which was also caked in every crease of my jeans. Other days Roger and I jumped our bikes off homemade ramps and proudly pedaled around the neighborhood, convinced we were the fastest and coolest riders around. Sometimes we'd go inside to concoct strange mixtures of household cleaners. I'm not sure why we did that. Perhaps we were waiting to see if something was flammable. Though that never occurred inside, we did unintentionally ignite a brush fire at the dead end down the block. We seemed to be on the same wavelength, both content with our symbiotic relationship. We played together and enjoyed the camaraderie that our nerdy selves didn't particularly attract at our separate elementary schools.

Otherwise, I often grabbed my basketball and withdrew outside. I never asked anyone else to play. Not even Roger. Eventually, I charted my own college basketball playoff brackets. I was all the players on both teams. I leaped to grab a rebound from my last missed shot. I dribbled around an outstretched defender. I passed the ball to myself for the final shot into our hoop bolted to the side of our house just outside Renee's room. My hours of bouncing that ball and announcing the games annoyed her to no end. But despite my short, scrawny non-athletic physique, I was a star forward and point guard in my fantasy world.

My fun alone times were somewhat blemished, given my mom's incessant prodding to find friends and my sisters' ribbing at my hours of basketball games and closet hideaways. After all, these were people I loved unconditionally. I might be able to brush off the needling of my classmates, but these concerns from my family confirmed these were not typical activities for a young boy. I got the message; something wasn't quite right.

CHAPTER 2: COCOON

I grew up in the '70s in Mountain Brook, Alabama, a suburb of Birmingham and a stark contrast to the city itself, which was still a tarnished town struggling to recover from its civil rights record of the '60s. In comparison, Mountain Brook lay within the rolling hills of lush grass, dogwood trees, chirping birds, and spacious red brick homes housing doctors, lawyers, and businessmen.

My folks moved into the Canterbury Gardens apartments in Mountain Brook after they married in 1956. My dad, Richard, was 28 and a business owner and mom, Sheila, 20, was a housewife. I was born ten years later, the youngest and only boy of a postcard crew of four kids. My sisters were two, four, and eight years older me. We moved to our house on Crestbrook shortly after I was born.

Despite my feelings of distance with others, I usually felt quite at home in the tranquility of our split-level. As the only boy in the family, I generally got along with my sisters, was spoiled rotten by my doting mother, and most admired and identified with my dad, who appeared to be a bit of a loner like me.

Dad had a business degree from the University of Alabama and, after serving in the US Air Force for three years during the Korean War, returned home to open a retail clothing business. Dad briefly operated Peter Pan Children's Store before shifting to his father's shop, Dixie Clothing Company in Bessemer, a steel town outside Birmingham where Dad grew up. I always sensed Dad was a simple man. While he towered over me in my youngest days, I could still tell that, compared to other adults, Dad was short in stature. He occasionally patted his modestly bulging midsection, silently bemoaning the lost buff physique of his Air Force days. However, dutifully, he did stretching exercises daily, spurred by his need to manage the stiffness and pain of a bad back. Dad had thinning black hair in his forties and occasionally sported a mustache or full beard, in part to cover up his vitiligo that left him with splotches of unpigmented light pink skin on his face and hands. Nevertheless, I can't recall Dad ever complaining about his own ailments, or his own burdens.

After Grandpa Izzy (Dad's father) died in 1969, Dad worked six days a week at Dixie Clothing, sacrificing a lot to provide for his growing family of six. On occasion, my sisters and I would help with semi-annual inventory or would just hang around the store on a Saturday or summer weekdays. The building was built in 1906 and was located on a prominent retail avenue in downtown Bessemer. The main floor, a maze of racked clothing for all ages set on a checkerboard of old red and black one-foot square tiles, welcomed the click-clack of high heeled shoes mixed with the shuffle of slippers worn by the diverse clientele come to visit "Mr. Dixie." The back section provided space for shoe inventory, with chairs and old metal foot-sizers.

But the upstairs was our favorite part. It housed paperwork and some old inventory and display racks and ran above the perimeter of the store like an oval running track. The space was mysterious yet familiar. It smelled of mothballs and was often dark, illuminated only by a few pull-string light bulbs on each side. There were jewels of old paraphernalia around each turn. We especially liked the places where we could slide a panel from the inside wall and peer down at all the activity on the shop floor below. Great memories for little kids.

In his little spare time, Dad was always with the family, helping Mom around the house and doing handiwork with his "helpers" at his well-stocked garage workbench. I could never remember a car parked in the cluttered and musty garage, though we did occasionally unfold the Ping Pong table and squeeze in a few matches. Dad was also a seasoned whistler. His cheeks would expand like a blowfish and then slowly deflate as he struck up "Bloody Mary" or some other show tune in the car or as he accompanied Mom's piano to their favorite musicals. Mom did an admirable job singing along. But the only time I ever heard Mom whistle was to call us kids from across the grocery or clothing store, with her trademark bird chirp.

Dad was a quiet guy, at peace in nature where he could escape the dueling pressures of business owner and patriarch. Every Thanksgiving, Dad and all us kids would head off with the Zimmermans, our cousins from across the state, to explore the outdoors through hiking, camping, and canoeing. Beyond those treks, Dad and I had the greatest opportunity to see nature together since I was the youngest and, frankly, the most available. However, I couldn't really appreciate his draw to nature. I was too young to recognize the bonding opportunities with my dad, preferring to stay home watching TV, playing basketball on the driveway, or riding my bike through the neighborhood for the afternoon. But Mom, who recognized my "mama's boy" persona and the distance it could create with Dad, coaxed me to join the hikes and thus I relented to spend time with him. I never wanted to disappoint my mother. However, to me, daylong hikes in the sticky, bug-filled woods presented long, boring hours away from my own hobbies. While I yearned for a male role model who could help guide me through my sense of being different, oddly, Dad couldn't fill that void. His own reserved nature made him the perfect candidate, yet it also thwarted him from approaching the subject and sharing his own private experiences. Our closeness seemed to be forced and superficial, hardly enough for me.

Despite my hidden apathy, Dad and I would tackle the trails of Cheaha State Park as well as the woods that lay just a few blocks out our back door. Our most frequent adventure was trekking to Peavine Falls at Oak Mountain State Park to watch the trickling waters and climb the rocks. When we got home, Dad would boast of my navigating skills and speed on the trails, mistaking my energy for enjoyment rather than my effort to hasten our return.

Since it appeared I loved the outdoors so much, Dad enrolled me in Cub Scouts. The campouts were a repeat of our Thanksgiving family excursions but with the laughs amongst cousins replaced by knot-tying and dreaded skits. Many of the other Cub Scouts appeared to be the odd, nerdy kids from my school. Though I never fit into the popular camp, I resisted acknowledging my placement amongst the geeks at school or in scouting. Scout meetings, badge events, and campouts intended to build camaraderie amongst kids, but they never drew me out of my quiet place.

However, the spring Pinewood Derby wooden model car race was a fantastic highlight. Dad and I worked for weeks perfecting our entry. Ours was a sleek, narrow car that weighed in just at the limit, thanks to many embedded ball bearings and countless coats of bright yellow paint. It was so much fun working on the car together, and I marveled at the attention to details in the design and weighting which Dad lent to the project.

"I can't wait to race, Dad," I called out from the back seat as we drove to the derby.

"Stephen, there are lots of other cars there. The chance of winning a ribbon is really small. Don't get your hopes up," Mom forewarned.

I glanced at Dad, hoping he would correct Mom and rekindle my optimism. That didn't happen. He just kept driving… silently. Hence, the anticipation of the big race was tempered by the feeling my parents didn't believe in me.

Nevertheless, once in the room I got caught up in the energy of the kids and dads darting around taking care of last-minute touchups and paperwork. Finally, the official called "Friedman," and I nervously placed my car at the top of the track. Once the other two cars were set, the release was pushed. I ran alongside as my car sped down the slope, clearly outdistancing my competitors and capturing a blue ribbon.

"We did it, Dad!" I beamed.

"Yes, son. We sure did. I'm so proud of you."

The excitement that Dad and I shared further escalated when we took home the shiny trophy for third place in design. It was great recognition for all the work we had put in.

I only had to endure one year of scouting. Perhaps both of us were happy to escape from the communal scene of meetings and campouts with strangers. Another deviation from my preferred solitude at home.

Meanwhile, Dad also had a passion for the theatre. He was a frequent and prominent actor in local Jewish Community Center musicals and plays including *South Pacific, Fiddler on the Roof,* and *Man of La Mancha.*

"I starred in the big spring musical at Bessemer High," Dad shared. "I've always loved the friends and fun of the theatre."

I thought he was so brave to be in front of all those people, remembering his lines and singing with such a broad smile on his face. Dad just seemed to beam onstage. It was like he pushed his concerns and reservations aside and got lost in the moment.

Occasionally, my middle sister Gayle would bring her bubbly personality to the stage with Dad, while Mom helped with the ticket sales and the rest of us cheered them on. Dad always sought to make everything a family event.

Other than a few fellow store owners in Bessemer, Dad's friends were few, but it didn't seem to bother him. He preferred quiet family time where he could relax. My dad had a dry, physical sense of humor. I think he was too reserved to know (or at least tell) too many jokes, but his goofy facial expressions were classics.

He had one gimmick he repeated for years, usually at the pleading of us kids and visiting relatives. Drawing from his theatrical prowess, Dad would get out his pretend needle and string. He'd spend about a minute trying to thread the imaginary needle, missing several times, next licking the thread, and cheering with a sly smile when he finally succeeded. He then aimed the threaded needle at his left pinky and jabbed it into the skin. Oh, how his face would grimace with excruciating pain as he pushed it deeper, and then hit bone! He had to push harder until the needle finally popped out the other end. After he panted a bit and wiped some sweat off his forehead, he proceeded to the next finger, each time gritting his teeth, grimacing, or letting out a bit of a gasp as he pushed his needle and string finally through his thumb. No matter how many times Dad put on the act, we all looked on intently, sometimes smiling and giggling, and other times grimacing and squinting right along with him. He had us wrapped around his needle-pierced fingers!

Once done, beaming with pride at his skill and pain tolerance, he exposed the string by spreading his fingers with a wide smile exposing his teeth to the audience. Afterwards, he reveled in the connectedness of the fingers and his pride in having survived the anguishing pain. I thought this was pure gold. Dad was the center of attention and he was in heaven. His brand of slapstick humor seemed to open doors in building relationships. As enticing and fun as that sounded to me, being the focal point performing in front of others scared me to death.

My mom, Sheila, grew up in the North, relocating around the country with her mother and siblings because of her traveling-salesman father, Leo. She lived in Chicago, LA, and Newark to name a few. In 1956, Mom was but 20, having just collected an associate degree in business from Fairleigh Dickinson University in New Jersey, before fate brought her family to Birmingham. Mom's gorgeous pin-up body later gave way to a more rotund figure in her forties. She had succumbed to the virtues of having four babies and leading a rather sedentary life. Most exercise came in the form of either grocery shopping for our expanding family or weekend garage-sale excursions, which yielded more knick-knacks and collectibles than our house could hold. As I grew up, tables and walls were adorned with mirrors, boxes, *chachkas*, and finally metal yard art when the house could hold no more.

I knew I was more like Dad than Mom. She was the more social of my parents, often on the phone with extended family, and arranging dinner and dancing with their local friends. She loved to chitchat but also felt compelled to adhere to the social norms within the community. Mom stayed home to take care of the four young kids, occasionally helping with the accounting books at Dixie Clothing.

Being the youngest, I have fond memories of Mom and me piling into our bright yellow station wagon with side paneling that looked like it came from our den. She spoiled me with toys as we walked hand-in-hand through Smith's Five and Dime and later played jacks on the front sidewalk waiting for Dad's Chevy Caprice Classic to top the hill, signaling his return from the day's work.

Otherwise, I would often spend time in the afternoon biking around the block. Inspired during the peak of Evil Knievel's spectacular jumps, I was a bit of a daredevil on my bike. Besides jumping off ramps with my friend Roger, I also managed to satisfy my unquenched need for attention by offering to two of my sisters that I would ride my bike as fast as I could down Crestbrook Road and straight into the big spruce bush across the street. They would just have to pay me a quarter each for the show. True to my word, I performed quite admirably, pumping my legs as I picked up speed coming down the block and finally plummeting into the big bush, hitting its hard core, and dropping out the side like a tree falling in the forest. I lay sprawled out on the street barely moving. It must have been quite a sight, as I recall my sisters running to get Mom. When she sprang out of the house to save her precious boy, she attended to my bruises and then inquired what my sisters, Renee and Gayle, were thinking—as if my stupidity was their fault. Mom insisted they pay up and admonished them for letting her baby do such a dangerous thing. My halo was well intact, and I was 50 cents richer!

However, my bravery was tested further one Saturday afternoon. With no one at our split-level house but Mom and me, I heard a shriek from upstairs. I sprang off the couch in the basement and bolted up a couple of flights of stairs, two steps at a time, while the panicked cries got louder. "Mom, are you okay?"

"Stephen, get up here quick. I need your help!" she pleaded.

Seconds later I arrived to find the screams were coming from the hall bathroom. I stood outside. "Mom, is everything okay? What's wrong?" I yelled through the door, concerned about what the answer might be and if I'd want to know.

"No, I need your help! Come in!" This, I feared, could be a life-altering moment. What was I going to find? Did I really want to go in?

But after one more pleading, I opened the door and slowly peered around the corner of the curtain-draped bathtub to find Mom standing on the top of the toilet, pointing at a large cockroach scurrying around the floor. Clearly she was scared, because the effort she exerted just to mount her 200-pound frame onto the toilet was an Olympic feat. To see her up there, shrieking "Get it, kill it!" was too much to handle. I dropped my hands to my knees exploding in laughter. After my enjoyment subsided, I smiled at my less than amused mother, and then put her, and perhaps the roach as well, out of their misery, thus restoring peace and quiet to the weekend.

But our house was actually rarely peaceful or quiet. Michelle was the oldest of the four, and the sister I knew the least since she moved out of the house to live with her long-haired boyfriend, Donnie, in 1974, when she was but sixteen and I was eight. I wasn't sure what that was all about. Mom and Dad didn't talk about it with me or anyone else that came over.

Gayle was four years my senior. She had light brown hair and was a bit taller than the rest of us. Gayle always appeared adventurous and confident to do her own thing. She was very creative and carefree, clearly in contrast to our parents more private demeanor.

Renee was only two years older than me. We played Barbies together, watched soap operas in the summer and reruns on school day afternoons. Squeezed between our rambunctious older sisters and my own angelic aura, Renee yearned for attention from Mom, but Mom didn't seem to have enough to spread around. They often appeared to be very similar: social and outgoing. Perhaps that was why they fought so much. Maybe because she was the third child, there were few baby pictures of Renee. My sisters joked that perhaps Renee was adopted, but our mirror-like facial features dispelled that more every year. Nevertheless, this added to the true anguish Renee felt. Sad and frustrated, this prompted Renee to go head-to-head with Mom on daily debates, which Mom was clearly unhappy to have yet equally determined to win. It created some scars that led Renee to seek the friendship and support she craved from outside the house. She often had a gregarious bounce to her step at school, sporting a beaming smile on her long face.

Renee and I shared many unforgettable moments together. I believe she was the only visitor to my special closet, where we played with Fisher-Price Little People for hours. Later we ventured outdoors for playtimes in our backyard and with neighbors. We laughed a lot, bringing joy to each other, perhaps filling our own personal voids.

I realized the bond Mom and I had was unique. As an innocent little kid, I could do no wrong by her. I was never apologetic for the connection we formed, but I was confused why my sisters couldn't get along with such a loving mother. Only later did I see that my sisters were at a very different stage in their lives, which seemed to bring out a sterner side of Mom. Or maybe that masked a more fragile aspect to Mom that only revealed itself later…

CHAPTER 3: CRESTBROOK

O ur house on Crestbrook Road was literally the only house I knew growing up. We moved there when I was about a year old. It stood as a rock throughout my youth and it provided comfort and love, too. Not just from the people within, but from the familiarity and warmth of the house itself.

Upstairs in our split-level house were four modest-sized bedrooms. Mine was the last on the L-shaped hallway, just next to my folks. My bedroom was cozy. There were two twin beds in the back corner, though I can never recall having a sleepover guest. My long dresser and desk were on opposite sides of the door. My desk was actually a converted old standup bar, with glass sliding doors on the top and a desktop that unlatched toward the chair. I hated that desk. It never could provide the space I needed. So, I usually crawled up into my closet to do my homework and hobbies.

When I joined the family downstairs, I often ran down the hall, turned the left corner, and easily leaped over the set of six stairs, being sure to nail the narrow landing to avoid hitting the coat closet door opposite. To the right was the blue linoleum floor and wallpapered front entryway walls leading to the living room. This area was adorned with Mom's trophies of royal blue and white Dutch Delft collectibles, which filled a tall, golden étagère. The walls were covered with Dad's cleverly mounted mirror creations along with Mom's needlepoints and bell-pulls. Despite the cushiony thick blue shag, whenever we walked through the living room, all the displayed *chachkas* would shake like glass Coke bottles in a wooden holder. The couch, a Frank Lloyd Wright original, was adorned with deep blue stitching and his trademark Taliesin carved wooden legs. The quaint house, bordering on tacky in places, was certainly not elaborate. Yet this Frank Lloyd Wright furniture was a showpiece which Mom and Dad were always so proud to highlight. Nestled between the Delft, mirrors, and needlepoint was Mom's upright piano, where her long nails clicked away to favorite show tunes. Dad would often pull out his clarinet and accompany Mom for several songs.

Around the corner lay a bland dining room used exclusively for Passover and Thanksgiving. Its narrowness necessitated sucking in stomachs and scooting behind filled chairs on tippy toes. But those holidays were my favorite meals. Both were filled with family and plenty of food, which together created an ambiance of relaxation and humor. Our Passovers devolved from a structured Seder dinner (Seder actually translates into "order") into one of devouring matzah, skipping sections of the service, and Dad sneaking an extra glass or two of tongue-smacking sweet Manischewitz wine for Prophet Elijah. The story says that Elijah joins the party through an open door and mysteriously drinks wine along with the family to celebrate the Israelites' miraculous escape from slavery in Egypt. So perhaps Dad was overplaying his part a bit. I marveled at how he craftily never got caught, despite attracting the frequent glares of us kids. As the youngest male, tradition appointed me to chant the Four Questions story at the table. I nervously began, soon to be spared as the whole family joined in during the chorus.

Our Thanksgivings customarily ended with Mom gnawing on the turkey neck and tushy and the other five of us stuffed turkeys recumbent on the living room floor, gradually recovering from gorging five different starches and four chocolaty desserts.

The dining room door opened to the equally cramped kitchen. It provided just enough space for the appliances along two walls with another full of pantry doors, behind which lay everything, but most importantly cereals and Pop Tarts. On the final side of our bright yellow wallpapered kitchen stood our table, which was rectangular, light brown, faux wood Formica with a leaf for expansion. The leaf remained out, given our large family, only removed once kids started to graduate from the home. In either case, the gap on both sides of the leaf tended to gather food and grease to make a somewhat sticky molasses adhesive that had to be scraped clean with a butter knife on a quarterly basis.

At the far corner of the kitchen lay the top of the steeper stairs to the basement. The bottom floor included the lonely bar nestled in the corner behind the steps. Faint memories of a couple of my parents' parties dimly remain. However, what really stood out was the transformative power of the free-flowing liquors from Dad's well-stocked bar during those rare gatherings. My otherwise reserved father benefitted as he schmoozed with the crowd. In front of the stairs and hugging the paneled wall was our L-shaped couch, providing a soft, warm landing in front of the heavy wood-console TV in the opposite corner. The TV was surrounded by the brick fireplace on the left side and the wide sliding glass door on the other.

Our beagle, Pokey, would often pull off our used gum that we'd plastered on the sliding glass door and chew it a bit before re-depositing it at the base of the door. Pokey was a staple of the house for years, along with our cuddly black and white cat, Shana, who often slept at the foot of my bed.

Dad usually closed the store around five and was home by six for dinner. Mom rang her Salvation Army-style bell to call all of us in from our outdoor playtime. Once seated, Mom tabled a well-balanced meal starring her favorites: brisket and potatoes, baked chicken over rice, lasagna, pork chops (an essential in a Southern Jewish home!), and occasionally the dreaded medley of chicken or calf's liver with rice, peas, and mushrooms. My personal challenge was how to minimize the intake of this horrid combination, spitting out some into my napkin when my parents weren't looking and stuffing my cheeks before excusing myself for a bathroom break to transfer more to the toilet. I can't imagine that my parents didn't see my trickery, but they let me continue while they kept on forcing liver to all of us. I must say it was the foulest thing I'd ever eaten. The textures remain lodged in my taste bud archives.

Our family dinner conversations tended to be as bland as the liver mix as we averted discussions on family finances, health, or my sisters' teenage adventures. Dad didn't like to share personal or work issues much, preferring to shield the kids and even Mom from reality while also avoiding conflict. Thus, superficial dinner conversations were largely a by-product of Dad's reserved and protective personality. I can't even recall discussing politics or world affairs, even in the tumultuous days of Watergate, the Cold War, and the Iran Hostage Crisis.

As my sisters peeled away after dinner for their social lives and telephone time, I joined my parents on the couch after homework was done for the night's TV sitcoms, Monday Night Football, or, like clockwork, the Olympics. Mom was perched in the corner, under our 10-globe silver light fixture, always busy with her reading or needlepoint while enjoying the company of the room. Dad and I lounged on each of the sides of the "L," often accompanied by the chocolate dessert of the night. We always seemed to have at least four forms of chocolate at home (ice cream, cookies, pie, brownies). My dad treasured one of his shirts, which read: "Give Up the Chocolate and Nobody Gets Hurt." It was not just a command, but a creed. Our sweets complemented the comfort of us hanging out, laughing at *Barney Miller, M*A*S*H, All in the Family, Taxi,* and *The Carol Burnett Show.*

By 10 PM on school nights, the three of us would head upstairs. After I changed into pajamas, I knocked on my parents' door for the customary goodnight wishes and peck on the cheek. This routine was so ingrained that if I forgot before I jumped into bed, I got up and knocked on their door to complete the ritual. This was home… this was the love I knew.

Our Saturdays were from days gone by. Usually Mom and Dad were at the store by the time my sisters and I woke before 9 AM. We ran downstairs, grabbing the box of chocolate Pop Tarts on the way, to claim our spot on the den couch. We laughed and stared at our favorite morning cartoons of *Laugh Olympics, Scooby Doo, Bugs Bunny,* and *Land of the Lost.* During commercials we dashed to complete our allocated chores around the house like cleaning the bathrooms, vacuuming, dusting, and straightening. But as long as we could catch the latest cartoons, Saturday morning was awesome.

Later in the afternoon, my sisters and I occasionally played kickball or King of the Mountain with our neighbors, Randy, Charles, and Hammond Snook, Jimmy Creamer, and big Johnny Miller from up the street. They were all my sisters' ages; none were really friends of mine. Other times I would go into our backyard, which sloped steeply away from the house before leveling out. On the flat section lay our jungle gym and my one-story fort made of 2x4 wood and supported by thousands of nails I'd pounded into all sides, exhibiting neither carpentry nor designer skills. I used the fort as another escape, though once Renee and I used it as our base for a rock-throwing war with the Snooks. (Note to Self: A rock-throwing war never ends well.) At the end of our backyard lay a concrete ditch, which split the Snook's and Roger's yard and flowed to the left into an underground sewer system that Roger and I sometimes played in—despite its very unsanitary and dangerously dark paths.

On autumn Sundays I was up early to drag the heavy newspaper into the house to frantically scan the sports section for college football scores and statistics. I tabulated all the data in my columnar pad which helped me prognosticate the next weekend's scores. It was a perfect solo hobby for me and my closet.

A bit later, after Dad crafted his family breakfast of fluffy biscuits, chocolate chip-laden pancakes, corned beef hash, or traditional matzah brei, he'd call everyone to the table with a playful shriek up the stairs, "Come and get it or I'll eat it myself!" Breakfast was always delicious and ended with Dad's plea for help in finishing the extras, a call which I usually succumbed to happily. Then, off to Sunday School at Temple Beth El. Myself inexplicably clad in a suit or, worse yet, pant suit to go with my nearly bowl-cut hairstyle—a perfect setup for the childhood teasing that awaited me.

CHAPTER 4: 4-5-9

In the late '70s, progress came to Birmingham. The city started to live up to its Magic City moniker, expanding from steel and coal to banking and medical while diversifying culturally and socially. Suburbs were growing, especially south from its core.

In 1977, at the age of eleven, my friend Roger and I wrote, typed, and "rented out" the first (and only) edition of *The Belle Meade News,* our little neighborhood's goings-on newsletter. Since we didn't have access to a copier, we only typed one original, thus necessitating a footnote in the word search on the Puzzle Page: "Please do not write on this page!" We managed to rent out *The Belle Meade News* three times (to our parents and one very kind neighbor, Mrs. Mills), bringing in 75 cents. As chronicled in an article, "Hi-Way Coming," the city's progress spurred infrastructure growth. Interstate 459, looping within a mile of our suburban home, stretched from Roebuck in the east to Bessemer in the west.

Dad especially lamented one section, which was so close to our home that the woods we had hiked were pared back to make way for concrete. As sections completed throughout the '70s, the new interstate acted as a magnet for development. People welcomed the short commute to new retail employment, while flocking to the Galleria Mall's shopping and social scene. Bessemer was part of that draw from only five miles away. As a result, Bessemer businesses—most certainly including my dad's store—suffered from the impact of competition as his customers began to migrate. Dad didn't discuss these concerns within the family, too proud to reveal the risks and too determined to protect our middle-class cocoon.

Nevertheless, the bills were racking up and the stress level within the family began to percolate. To alleviate some pressure, Mom began working at the local Sun Newspapers in their accounts payable department. This provided her with renewed challenges and social connections, but perhaps a sense of guilt as three of us became latchkey kids. At 11, I still yearned to recapture the special times with Mom, but her job accelerated my transition into adolescence. My afternoons became marathons of '70s reruns enveloped by the couch downstairs. While I was still a harmless pre-teen, my sisters were at various stages of teenagerhood.

Michelle, at 19, was still enjoyed her wild years experimenting with pot and other drugs of the times. We reconnected at family dinners and when Renee and I helped her move to new houses. Gayle, at 15, was confident, caring, and a bit revolutionary, as she prepared to get her driver's license—her ultimate step toward greater independence. Gayle, too, tried various drugs during high school, though seemingly under Mom and Dad's radar. Renee, only 13, might have appeared to be the calmer sister, except the unrequited affection she yearned for continued to present challenges mixing with Mom, as both were a bit proud and argumentative. This all made for constant bickering and more frequent yelling up and down the stairs. Mom and Dad had just finished funding a lavish Bat Mitzvah for Renee, their third in six years, and saw my Bar Mitzvah on the horizon in 1979. The stress level noticeably ratcheted up at home.

While Mom and Dad worked long days, I struggled with my body image. My short height and extra weight both contributed to my low self-esteem. Throughout my school yearbook, classmates addressed me as "small fry" and "Porky," signing with comments like "for a little fella, you shure [sp] are smart," and "don't think of yourself too big, little one!" At my parents' suggestion, I even tried growth hormones to boost my height toward the normal range. This did more damage in underscoring the issue than actually fixing the problem.

Meanwhile, my lack of social confidence, when combined with my stocky status, made it difficult to gather the courage to make new friends. Whether guys or girls, I was often stuck not knowing what to talk about. My fears of embarrassment and failure kept me from even attempting many such engagements.

My first crush was in third grade on Caroline Egea down the street. It fizzled out before it really got started. We awkwardly conversed at school but, after our first play date at her house, her mammoth Great Dane punctured our relationship by attacking my 90-pound frame, raising the prospect of rabies shots until their dog was tested negative. This was taken as a sign for both of us to move on. Thereafter, my childhood crushes tended to be from afar… Meanwhile, though I remained a dog lover with Pokey having been replaced by Klutz and Charlotte at home, this crisis foreshadowed further dog clashes to come.

At 10 and in fifth grade at Cherokee Bend Elementary School, my life became more complicated. I was always an "A" student, but as social cliques formed in those pre-teen years, I seemed to frequently be on the outside. Being relegated to second-class was easy to see, but tough to accept. Some of the other outsiders and I found ourselves huddling together during playground recess, plotting against the popular elementary fraternity. It was, sadly, my first leadership experience, gathering up the group at recess, and yet it still didn't cultivate the social interaction or confidence I was seeking. Though we never clashed, the mere existence of such groups represented the new social pressures and frustrations which pre-teen years were set to introduce.

In the spring of '77, at 11, my curiosity met temptation while enjoying rare solitude at home. I can't recall plotting out my venture into Dad's bar. I wasn't waiting for weeks or even days for an empty house to implement any devious plan, but perhaps I was yearning for something to quench the mounting stress at home or the feeling of personal awkwardness and discomfort at school. Maybe this presented an opportunity to grow up within a house full of new grown-up issues. The thought just flashed before me on one of my first nights home alone. As I walked down the steps and approached the bar, I rationalized that my older sisters had certainly experimented, and I was almost a teenager, so why not me?

Dad was never much of a drinker and no longer seemed to have use for the dusty bar as an entertainment venue, perhaps a marker of my parents' more social days gone by. Nevertheless, the bar was still full of glasses and fancy bottles of well-aged liquor. I had no idea what any of it tasted like or how to mix a drink, but the decorative bourbon decanter with the blue Marlin fish plastered across the front had always looked inviting up on the shelf.

Reflecting the clash of eras, I took an eight-ounce jelly jar that had once been used to offer preserves for family breakfasts to receive a warm, straight shot of whisky. I slowly dipped my tongue in, pulling it back quickly from the sweet yet stinging taste. I tried another dip, and then a sip. As I walked around the empty house, I began to surrender to the soothing warmth building deep in my stomach.

Eight ounces of straight bourbon was a lot, especially for a young kid, all of 4'10" and 100 pounds. I didn't remember finishing the glass before throwing up and passing out on my parents' bed, apparently eager for their attention despite the wrath I was sure to receive.

"What have you done? What's wrong with him, Richard?" I heard my mom rattle off. "I'll call the doctor. Stephen, sit up! Oh my God. Richard, did he take pills?"

As I awakened on Dad's side of their bed to this clamor, I saw him sniffing my empty glass on the floor. "He drank some bourbon, Sheila. Get a washcloth and some water and crackers."

"Dr. Kartus, it looks like Stephen had quite a lot of bourbon," my mom shrieked into the phone. "No, I don't think he had anything else. Does he need to go to the hospital? Yes, he threw up a lot!" After a pause, she finished "Okay, Dr. Kartus, thanks," and she hung up the phone.

"It looks like most of it is out of his system. A cold shower and some crackers should help."

I was groggy from the late hour and certainly the effects of my first drink as it lapsed into my first hangover… at the age of eleven. Dad carried me into the shower and then put me to bed, warning "We will talk about this in the morning, young man!"

Sunday morning rolled around, and my empty stomach followed the wafting smell of biscuits and bacon down to the kitchen. I sat in my designated chair, receiving stares from my parents and inquisitive, somewhat respectful smirks from Gayle and Renee. "How do you feel?" Mom broke the silence.

"Okay," I murmured, head down.

"What were you thinking?" Dad interjected.

"I just wanted to try some. That's all."

"We'll talk later," my dad cautioned again, and returned to the oven to check on the biscuits. We never did talk about it again… ever! And Mom never brought it up either, likely nervous to put our lifelong bond to the test. Suddenly, instead of observing the stresses of the family around me, overnight I had become the newest contributor.

A year and a half later, months of practice culminated in my successful and memorable Bar Mitzvah on February 24,

1979. A Bar Mitzvah is a Jewish rite of passage for 13-year-old boys, culminating after years of studying the history and traditions of the Jewish people at Sunday School and learning to read and sing Hebrew on Wednesday afternoons.

Over the weekend, I led most of the service chanting prayers and traditional songs in Hebrew before closing the ceremony sharing a speech about myself with the hundreds of guests. For just a couple of hours on the *bimah*, or stage, at our synagogue that Friday and Saturday, I was transformed from a shy, pudgy, nearly 13-year-old with pitch problems to a confident young man. By the time service was over, I stood tall on the *bimah* with a beaming grin of pride and satisfaction. I had applied my months of preparation to command the stage with onlookers, including friends and family who traveled from across the country to kvel, kibbitz, and nosh.

That evening we hosted the traditional Friedman Bar Mitzvah party at The Club, a posh venue offering a fancy meal and a large dance floor. These events tended to be more for the parents than the Bar Mitzvah. Ladies were wearing their fanciest dresses and guys donned suits and ties. After a nice sit-down dinner, lights turned low and the dancing began. I wasn't particularly friends with my Bar Mitzvah class attendees, whom I'd known since kindergarten, and my few school friends and I, as 12- and 13-year olds, were not much for the paired-up dance scene. If I'd been asked, I'd rather have had a small bowling, skating, or go-cart party. So I stood off to the side with the other pre-pubescent boys, mumbling and staring at the distant girls.

Dad had recently decided to close the business, after a few rough years, and Mom was clearly feeling the stress of work and teenage struggles. This was a parent party, for them to celebrate the end of my practice and performance, but also to reconnect with distant relatives, and temporarily escape the mounting stress of everyday life.

Caught between the waning pride of my synagogue performance and a deepening sense of boredom, I asked Dad if I could have a drink. He smiled, "You are a man now (according to Jewish tradition). You can have *one* drink." He led me to the bar and he ordered a Screwdriver. Though he didn't say much, his smirk suggested he was treating this as a good opportunity to present me a more palatable taste, as he recalled my bourbon choice a couple of years earlier.

Slowly the social stresses drifted away. I floated around the room and mingled with the crowd. I enjoyed the fun a bit more, especially after sneaking a second and third unsupervised cocktail. In retrospect, perhaps my parents should have been firm and insistent, but they were exhausted from the experimenting of my three older sisters and didn't appear to have the energy, especially that night. That evening's foray certainly felt better than my initial drinking disaster, and this time I felt the calming nature of a few drinks in a social situation.

CHAPTER 5: DELICATE

Turbulent family conditions provided a traumatic backdrop to my teenage years. Dad was working for someone else for the first time since his Air Force days three decades earlier. It was clear he was unhappy selling retail jewelry, and with the physical strain that standing all shift was having on his aching mid-50s frame, but even worse were the nights and weekends Dad had to work. He was doing his duty to provide yet sacrificing family time to do so—it was tearing him apart.

Perhaps under the weight of stress from three liberated teenage girls and a son prepared to test boundaries as well, combined with the financial hardships of the family, Mom became increasingly sad and removed. They never went out socially anymore and she spent more time in their room. I would often hear my folks arguing behind closed doors, late at night. Was the '80s divorce trend coming to our family? Was someone sick? Were financial problems becoming overwhelming? These possibilities scared me. I loved my parents and needed them. I ached to hear what they were talking about, but only if it would dismiss my fears.

All I knew was that it rattled my perfect world and scared me into tears many nights. I didn't care that it was such a raw moment. I felt like my world was crumbling around me every time they argued. I cried from the sadness of their anger and stress. I cried because of the unsettling changes to our house. I cried for the perfect childhood lost in the distance. Often, I made sure I sobbed loud enough to attract Mom's attention.

This seemed to accomplish two objectives: Mom would come in to reassure me "everything will be all right," and they would stop fighting—at least until I fell asleep. But I knew things weren't all right. My warm cocoon was frayed. I constantly feared this love and security was being ripped away, just as my expanding physique and narrowing social life chipped away at my own self-confidence.

Meanwhile, my time with my pal, Roger Bates, came to an abrupt halt. Roger had been zoned to a different elementary school, but when we started going to the same middle school the very things that had kept us together began to pull us apart. We had shared so many childhood hobbies: cars in the dirt, neighborhood newsletter, jumping ramps on our bikes. But maybe I couldn't transform into the more popular teen I yearned to be without shedding my nerdy past and moving on separately? So, I opted to shun him and make fun of his last name ("Master Bates") rather than exhibit the courage to embrace our years of true friendship and adventure. I treated him poorly and, as a result, lost one of my true childhood friends just when I needed him most.

Despite my parent's urging, weekends were still filled with solo games of basketball, college football stats, stamp collecting (which my Grandpa Leo had introduced me to), and unaccompanied neighborhood biking adventures. I sensed this reclusive lifestyle was not quite normal, yet I wrapped myself in this solitude.

My loving parents hardly provided me with all the necessary tools to manage the stress of everyday life and its twists and turns. I was armed with an appetite far exceeding my short frame, an intense love for chocolate, a proclivity for a sedentary lifestyle, and thus an aversion to physical exercise. Meanwhile, I was swimming in an atmosphere that bottled up emotions, concerns, worries, and sadness rather than developing the skills to share and cope.

Husky! I think I was about 11 when I got my first husky size pants. I was falling prey to the Friedman family curse of stress eating, and celebration eating, and clock eating. By 15 these eating problems were growing and impacting others. My dad's mother, Grandma Ray, began living with us as her dementia became untenable. I had gorged on a whole pie from the fridge one day. My parents noticed and asked who had eaten the pie. I didn't raise my hand, instead letting my parents lay blame on my innocent, defenseless grandmother. What a disgraceful way to deal with stress. I'd hoped this would be a low point which would shake me to a higher moral ground, but that was not the case.

As with most husky boys, I hated gym class. All the intimidating and demeaning competition with those much more gifted than me. Oh, how I yearned for square dancing or calisthenics to the tune of "The Youth Fitness Song," better known to students in the '70s and '80s as the "Chicken Fat" song. When given the opportunity to opt out of athletic skill competitions like baseball, I did so. This led to my first near-death experience.

One day in middle school, Greg Aldrete and I secured a pass from baseball to walk laps around the athletic field. We lost ourselves in conversation as practices and exhibitions occurred around us. Suddenly, Greg pushed me to the ground, saving me from a searing javelin heading straight toward me! I jumped up and thanked Greg for his efforts, and we resumed our path, chuckling at the prospect of becoming a human shish kabob. After several more laps, Greg rescued me once again as he shoved me away from a spinning metal discus that surely would have broken some bones at the very least. Those are a couple of my most poignant athletic memories.

In my family, we were consistently sedentary without any natural inclination toward sports or exercise. Dad did lots of stretches and walking for decades to take care of his back and stiff joints, but otherwise, no one was hitting the gym or playing sports beyond the failed attempts at tee-ball and toddler gymnastics. When I was in high school, Mom coaxed me to go out around 5 AM to walk and jog the neighborhood with Dad. I felt like a speed demon, though in actuality I was only outpacing a 55-year-old man who had lost his form years ago. After gaining some confidence, I signed up for the high school cross country squad, only to realize after the first scorching August afternoon practice that running—a LOT of running—was involved. That was my one and only day on the team. Thus far in my life I hadn't really exhibited much fortitude.

Meanwhile, Mom spiraled into what I could only later describe as a state of depression. Over the next couple of years, she continued to work but struggled to attend to her duties at home. She thought she was going crazy. This must have been quite a struggle for her. Dad's work schedule made it difficult for him to help around the house or with Mom's condition. Meanwhile, Gayle headed off to college and Renee was in her senior year of high school. Though our personalities were so different, Renee and I remained close. She seemed to be a bit of my alter ego. She gave me unsolicited tips about girls, helped me break into our house when we both forgot our keys after school, mentored my high school journalism ambitions, and forewarned me that "if you don't stop eating so much, you'll look like big Johnny Miller up the street."

Somehow, I continued to plow through my high school years. I became even more of a loner, sinking into my homework and homebound hobbies. Maybe this was normal teenagerhood for people. However, given that my reserved father wasn't around much anymore, and without any brothers or close friends, I just didn't know how to assess that. I drudged on through high school until suddenly I was 16 and embraced the solitude, responsibility, and freedom which came with my driver's license.

I was able to get an afternoon job at my parents' friend's office, doing paperwork and filing for their burial garment business. Bizarre, yes, but apparently there is a whole industry based on the fact people would rather bury their loved ones in strange new clothes rather than their favorite shorts and flip flops. One of the factory workers indoctrinated me the first week by hiding in a coffin they were lining in the warehouse, springing out to scare me half to death. They thought I might need that very coffin for me as a result.

I enjoyed the work and the spending money it provided and was able to get my first car—a 1973 Ford Comet, which I bought from my sister, Michelle. It was nothing fancy; gold that had faded to tan with a peeling leather roof and my battery-powered radio covering for the broken car stereo. But the independence was nice and provided an escape from the household melancholy.

Mom was barely leaving the house now. This was not the same Mommy that had played jacks on the sidewalk and who took me to the five and dime for a toy. In 1982 Renee headed off to college. Suddenly, I was all alone. As Mom got worse, she was gone for several weeks at a mental hospital for the help we all knew she required. I was still not sure what the issue was, and the stigma of mental illness made it difficult for my parents to discuss or cope. I visited her daily after my afterschool work. I don't recall us really talking about what she was going through or how she was feeling. I just sat with her and gave her updates of home and school.

In my effort to lighten the mood, I put on a scene to pretend to shampoo her hair. She would giggle with a girlish grin when I came up behind her while she was seated in her chair facing the mirror. I pulled my cheeks out with each hand and shook them back and forth to make a watery sound that mimicked squeezing the last of the shampoo out of the bottle. Then I proceeded to massage the shampoo into her scalp. Later I added facial expressions that showed my quirkiness and all-in dedication to the moment, occasionally also lending my Brooklyn Yenta impression to the scene: "Oy vey, bubby! Such a head of hair on you!" I repeated my act for Mom, sometimes with a family audience. I was stealing a page from Dad's comedic playbook, though I was not pulling it off with such magnificence. Others chuckled, but no one enjoyed it like Mom.

Over time, a new doctor finally helped Mom. He diagnosed her with agoraphobia. For some this disorder appears as a fear of the outdoors or crowds. For Mom, it was the anxiety of being trapped in enclosed places like restaurants or airplanes. Unbeknownst to me, she had been tormented by this fear since I was six! The effect of the undiagnosed phobia, combined with her efforts to hide these panic attacks from her family and friends, created tremendous stress on Mom. Not only did she lose her own stability, but her social calendar was scrubbed clean. How tragic. My mom, a talkative, social, outgoing person was terrified to go out with people or even family.

Finally, the meds and therapy helped Mom to return home to recuperate and start on the road to recovery. After learning how to cope with her own anxiety, Mom eventually mentored others afflicted with agoraphobia in Birmingham. However, she would never quite be the same, scarred by years of depression that for decades she feared was not far from returning.

I sure wish she had shared her struggles and triumphs with me at the time. It would have replaced the air of mystery and fear with an aura of trust, strength, and courage. How inspiring would that have been for a reserved, rudderless teen like me?

Mom, now 46, was gaining weight, her hair was graying more rapidly than she could dye her roots, and her soft face was beginning to droop from sadness. She stayed in more, traveled less, and lacked the confidence that she had carried so well. My sturdy, forceful, fun mom was now delicate.

CHAPTER 6: ESCAPE

Meanwhile, the neighborhood games with the Snooks disappeared as they joined my sisters in escaping to college. Instead, I would spend weekends with school friends Steven and Allen, usually at Steven's house, checking out this new TV channel, HBO, in hopes we would occasionally get a shot of grainy breasts on a midnight movie. We did venture out at times, occasionally buying liquor to make strange concoctions like Vodka and Mello Yellow, then driving the neighborhood looking for trouble. Our excursions involved an occasional TP-run (draping toilet paper over trees), brown bag drop (leaving a brown bag full of dog crap in front of someone's door and ringing the bell), or bottle rocket shooting (from the end of a plastic bat) as we sped around the neighborhood in my tan Comet.

Unfortunately, this newfound independence was not without its risks. I lost control of my car once, plowing into some small pine trees across a median before resting on the other side facing traffic, my face white with fear having narrowly averted diving into a cavernous ravine on the road's edge. While this was due to high speed and recklessness rather than drinking, driving under the influence was becoming a common condition. I never really felt we were skirting the law or being dangerous. We were 17 and invincible! What else were we going to do? We were too young to get into bars except for one: Sammy's Go Go.

As the name might suggest, Sammy's was a titty bar, or—as others tried to upgrade it—a gentlemen's club. But this was really no gentlemen's club. When we walked in, we were placed at a small, wobbly round table with ripped chairs. I sensed there were filthy, sticky, peeling walls behind the constant darkness. But Sammy's had a few things going for it: they accepted our novice fake IDs, they had scantily clad women performing their pole acrobatics, and they sold cheap beer. We occasioned Sammy's only a few times, feeding our burgeoning libidos and our thirst for beer.

Despite growing up surrounded by women, my childhood nerves around girls remained through high school. Perhaps *because* I grew up with so many older women in the house, I knew a lot about their temperament, hormones, and hygiene, and it either intimidated me or completely turned me off. I don't know which. But my teen years were basically void of dating, kissing, or fraternizing with girls.

Occasionally, I would spend some time on weekends with my sister Michelle, catching up or having her boyfriend Leslie repair the latest issues with my Comet. Michelle was back in school pursuing her accounting degree. However, when I came to visit, it felt like what I imagined Woodstock to be. Cigarettes and alcohol were the norm. There wasn't guzzling, so characteristic of us teenagers who were just surprised to be drinking a beer and constantly worried about being busted. It was just a chilled atmosphere with their friends gathered in the den, talking and laughing as they lit up bongs and passed them around the room. I had never tried pot in any form and so I declined the offers. I hadn't even had a cigarette. It was a strange, bizarre world that both scared me and gave me a false sense of comfort that my beer drinking with friends was tame and harmless. I didn't visit Michelle often, perhaps concerned that my conviction was not strong enough to handle much temptation. I preferred when she came to the house for dinner or when the two of us spent a few days on the white, sandy beaches of the Florida panhandle together one summer. It was a fun time to bridge our eight-year gap and get to know each other a bit better.

Throughout high school I'd been writing for our school newspaper, *The Sword & Shield,* and eventually followed Renee as co-editor. The paper provided me with a little cave of co-workers within a loud, preppy high school. I liked the writing and excitement of printing a paper every week. I also enjoyed attracting the "oohs" and "aahs" from impressed classmates during my in-class interview with the school quarterback.

"How do you do that?" one remarked.

"What?" I asked.

"Taking notes without looking at your notebook."

"Oh, it's nothing," I blushed. Their reaction seemed genuine though misguided, given there was no mention of my journalistic skill itself. Nevertheless, I was a sucker for even the smallest degree of recognition.

The summer before my senior year I attended Journalism Camp at the University of Alabama in Tuscaloosa. This was my one and only sleep-away camp as a kid. I'd never been interested in traditional summer camps. Days away from the comforts of home with strangers, doing team-building and sports? But I was excited about this camp. It presented a chance to learn more about journalism and writing, to see how this passion might grow. I soaked up some of the tricks of the trade, met other high school journalists from across the South, and published an interview with a 'Bama assistant football coach in the camp paper. It was exciting, productive, and encouraging.

The camp also served as a bit of a lure for the university to attract high school seniors. I didn't need any such enticement.

I was a diehard Alabama fan with the 'Bama legacy of my dad and two of my sisters, Renee and Gayle. I was 'Bama bound since the age of two, when I could yell "Roll Tide."

The camp also offered career and personality tests to provide some insight toward college majors, which was most helpful given my underdeveloped ambitions. The career survey pointed toward business or journalism. The personality test evaluated tendencies and comfort zones, ultimately assessing subjects on an introvert-extrovert continuum. This concept was new to me. It placed me clearly on the extrovert wing of the bell-shaped curve, more sociable, gregarious, and quick-witted than reserved, thoughtful, or creative. I was surprised at the results, since they seemed in stark contrast with my real personality. Nevertheless, at week's end I returned home to discuss my post-high school plans with my folks.

Given the fervent Cold War rhetoric of the Reagan Era, we had a brief discussion about the prospect of enlisting in the US Army, in part to avoid the more dangerous front lines reserved for draftees. This approach mirrored the path Dad took in the Air Force in the early years of the Korean War, but didn't really seem necessary in 1984. The topic thankfully faded with the possibility of a new draft looming, enlisting in order to contribute from the relative safety away from the front lines was an important consideration, mirroring the path Dad took in the Air Force in the early years of the Korean War. We didn't really debate or argue, but they raised legitimate concerns and I listened. However, that topic thankfully faded, leaving us to focus conversations on what I'd major in at the University of Alabama.

I led off by sharing my interest in continuing to write through a journalism degree at Alabama. However, scarred by their own money struggles, Mom and Dad saw a business degree as a path to financial security, more so than journalism.

Despite the gratification I got writing for the high school paper and the notoriety it provided a shy, innocuous boy like me, I never fought for my passion in journalism. Perhaps I never even acknowledged it as a passion at that point. Heck, I was 17. I had no great convictions, and I surely didn't recognize the significance of the decision—not just for my college years, but for my career and my peace of mind along the way. Frankly, I just wanted to drink beer and dream of finally moving to college, away from the house that had become a bit sad and lonely, especially since Renee had gone. My blinding respect for my parents' authority left me to register as a business major and count down my final months at home.

High school ended much the way it started. Solid As, Dad still frustrated at work, and Mom recovering a bit but far from herself. As senior summer hit, my two best friends, Steven and Allen, headed to 'Bama to settle in for summer school. I reconnected with an old friend, Lee Phillips. Lee was a big burly guy, nice, fun, a big ZZ Top fan, but a bit rudderless. Despite decent grades, he had quit high school and was working at the neighborhood Western Supermarket. We quickly began the tradition of partying on Saturday nights, parked near his quiet neighborhood, talking, dreaming and complaining about life in general with a 12-pack of beer until about midnight.

In June I asked my parents for permission to escape to St. Petersburg, Florida for a week long vacation with Lee and his friend Paul. Our plans were few: drink, go to the beach, and ride the rides at Busch Gardens. Surprisingly, Mom and Dad relented. At the last minute Lee had to beg off so Paul and I, nearly strangers, drove to St. Pete. The next day we met a couple of girls on the beach and got to talking. We enjoyed each other's company, talking, flirting, and drinking. It all seemed very bizarre to me, but the distance from Birmingham and the constant flow of beer provided some detachment from my reserved, meager self.

The four of us spent the rest of our week together. I had paired up with Lena, an Asian girl from Belize, and we soon found ourselves holding hands and walking the beach. I'd never had such a connection in my life. We had fun together and became each other's first sexual encounter. It was a clumsy, fumbling moment that really meant nothing yet everything in the world. I returned to Birmingham with a bit of a confident swagger.

It was all fun until a fateful July night when I was brought down a peg.

Lee and I had just polished off a 12-pack while parked at a dark dead end, and separately headed home. I knew I shouldn't be driving, but I'd done it many times before without any problems. I was young and invincible, after all. I coached myself into driving slow and straight. I was five miles from home. A few turns later, on the winding roads of our hilly, upscale neighborhood, I realized someone had been following me for several blocks and turns.

Who could it be? Am I in danger?

Their bright lights glared at my face through the rearview mirror.

I need to stop them! How long have they been following me?

My heart pounded as they seemed to get closer.

I need to lose them!

I slid through the next stop sign and took an abrupt left turn on to Maryland Avenue and stared in the mirror. The next move was theirs.

When those red flashing lights came on, all the pieces quickly came together like an all-too-simple jigsaw puzzle. I pulled over and soon joined the officer in his black-and-white squad car, grasping the cracked back seat cushions and staring through the mesh metal barrier between us. During that short ride to the police station, my mind darted in and out. Was there any way to get out of this? What was next?!

Since I was only 18, with the fresh, innocent look of someone much younger, the police in our cozy town sat me in a chair in the hall and told me to call my dad. "Dad, I ran a stop sign and now I'm at the Mountain Brook Police Station. Can you come pick me up?" I think I'd rather have been handcuffed, fingerprinted, and put in a cell for the night than forced to explain to my dad what really happened.

But there he was, 30 minutes later, about 20 yards down the long hallway, headed my way, with his head steadily getting bigger, framed by the small square window on the door between us. By the look of determination in his face and the pace of his walk, I could tell he knew the whole story. My fear was not that Dad would be physical or abusive. Far from it. My fear was more from guilt. My dad had so much on his mind, had done so much to provide for our family, and I was letting him down. Not that this could be considered too surprising. My path had been leading to this point for years. Once Dad pushed the door open and walked to me, he said more with his facial expressions and silence than with his voice.

We talked very little about what happened. Heart-to-hearts with my parents just didn't really occur, so I was left to cope as best I knew how. I returned home that night to process the events alone. I was broken and swore to myself never to put my parents through that again.

However, just two weeks later, I came back from another night out with Lee and passed out on my bed. So much for my well-intentioned promise. My parents were shocked to find me clearly disheveled and they woke me fuming. They accused me of drinking or smoking pot and their warranted anger instilled a deep sense of remorse. After a very short conversation I returned to bed to sleep it off.

In the morning, my conscience weighed heavily. But rather than introduce a conversation I was not raised to have, I turned to writing a letter. I tried to explain myself with lies to appease them: "I had only three beers last night. I was not drunk and did not drive drunk. I think I learned my lesson two weeks ago."

However, the whole episode showed poor judgment on my part. I was so torn between doing what was right and enjoying the escape which drinking beer with Lee afforded me that I continued to lie to my parents. I concluded my one-page letter: "I'm so sorry. Y'all are so good to me and I don't want to hurt you." We never discussed my letter, though I did find it decades later, buried in my Mom's drawer amongst all the other letters, postcards, and report cards she had collected from her kids.

For the balance of the summer, I was overcome with guilt and confused by my inability to self-correct. I spent more time alone in my room, rarely joining my parents downstairs to watch TV amidst a different, more tense level of silence.

As my departure for college drew near, I was nervous that the social pressures of my new environment would lead me to rely upon my drinking habits to cope, as I had these last few years. I realized this was not the smart path, but I knew of no other way to calm my fears.

By mid-August, my parents and I seemed to be exhausted and relieved to take a break from each other. I sold the Comet for cash and headed to Tuscaloosa.

SECTION TWO – SAVED

CHAPTER 7: LANTERN

I finally arrived at the University of Alabama in Tuscaloosa, just an hour southwest of Birmingham. The campus appeared serene, with a sprawling grassy quad in the middle that was crisscrossed with sidewalks and huge live oaks aligning the perimeter. As a freshman I lived at Rose Towers, an apartment-style high-rise dorm about a half-mile down the hill from the quad. I shared a suite with my high school buddies, Steven and Allen. The familiarity of friends was calming for my first several weeks.

On my way back from a day of classes not long after my first semester started, I made a grand entrance into Rose Towers. Powering my bike from campus down the hill, I swerved wide left to glide into the parking lot when I hit some gravel on the road. Instantly I was sprung off my bike and slid face-first on the asphalt like a baseball player stealing second base. After shaking off the cobwebs, I surveyed the area only to find a busload of elementary students watching the entire scene from across the street. Some were in awe of the slide and others sent an uproarious laugh out the bus windows toward me. Beaten and embarrassed, I picked up my twisted bike and hobbled to my apartment. I spent the next couple of hours with my sister Renee at the infirmary where the campus nurse used tweezers to extract countless pieces of asphalt and gravel from my arms and legs. What remained were deep scrapes, which a classmate and I stared at during biology class, tracing blood moving within the capillaries just a few thin layers below the new surface of my arm. It seemed ghoulishly appropriate for biology and not the last time I'd be having irreconcilable differences with asphalt.

While many were busy pledging fraternities, the reputation of subservience and social pressures in Greek life were a bit daunting and unappetizing to me. The convenience, ease, and camaraderie of dorm life lured me in. My weekends typically focused on utilizing my fake ID to sneak into college bars or hanging out in the dorm with others who managed to acquire beer one way or another. Alabama certainly drew a diverse set of people from across the state and the South. One of my first acquaintances was Tina Wall from Arab (pronounced with a strong first "A") in remote northern Alabama. A seemingly nice girl with a heavy southern twang, when she discovered I was Jewish she remarked, "I've heard of you people. Where are your horns?" She was serious. I was not in Mountain Brook anymore.

Another dorm mate was Sondra, a freshman from the southern edges of the state. It didn't appear we had much in common, but she was a blonde knockout who had me more than smitten. One weekend, we enjoyed several drinks together after which she invited me to her dorm room. She got under the covers and peeled her clothes off, throwing them across the room. I was mesmerized, perplexed, and excited! She invited me into the bed, but then made no further advances. Nervous and unfamiliar with this scene, I lay in the bed with clothes on debating my options until Sondra passed out. Bewildered, I slinked out of the room, somewhat proud I had passed some moral proving ground but confused by the mixed signals of my first college encounter—not to mention frustrated by my unsatisfied libido.

After these dramatic introductions to college life, I settled into a dual life at Alabama, precariously balanced like a seesaw. I became intensely diligent at my academic and work obligations yet tested new boundaries of social freedom. The astuteness came from my dad who was an exemplar for hard work, responsibility, and pride. I wanted to make him proud, but more so I was developing high standards and expectations for myself. I wanted to do well. Grades were important. I'd heard many examples of freshman excuses as their grades ran into the ground. I was determined not to be another statistic.

The new rigor of college classes energized me to adhere to a structured regimen of typing class notes on my Tandy-Radio Shack computer with dot matrix printer, and re-reading chapters and notes before each test. High school had usually required an hour or two of homework a night. My drive to excel in college forced me to develop both organizational and time management skills. My grades reflected such dedication. My work ethic focused on studies in the evenings before making time for drinking at the residence hall or out at the bars late at night.

College provided an incubator to develop myself academically and socially, a playground free from parental oversight and the stresses of our Birmingham home. Thus, despite my fresh initiative (or perhaps in part because of it), accelerated drinking helped me manage my persistent social anxiety.

In order to support my drinking tab, I pursued a new hobby through a friendly acquaintance as a sports bettor and bookie my sophomore year. Having been immersed in college football news, statistics, and prognostications throughout my teens, I began placing small wagers. Soon I was working for my contact bringing other students into the fold. It was edgy and exciting. Both my frequent wins and growing reputation within the ring provided a weekly adrenalin rush. As the fall season progressed, my bets eventually grew to hundreds of dollars each weekend. I spent hours researching games and even more time monitoring scores on Saturday. It became a rollercoaster ride of emotions as my involvement built.

However, as my new habit grew beyond my means, this was becoming a risky and potentially dangerous venture. Toward the end of the season, I ran into a streak of bad luck. With that, the cordiality of my bookie and the respect of others involved vanished. These were not friends, just business counterparts. While I was able to cover my losses, I feared there would come a point where I would not be able to control myself. At the end of the season, just in time for my return to Birmingham for Christmas break, I pulled out completely.

Home for a few weeks, I huddled with my parents to address my academic direction. "I need to declare a major soon before I sign up for fall classes. I'm just not sure what to choose. How do they expect me to know what I want to do for the rest of my life after three semesters?"

"It's a big decision, Steve," Mom interjected. "What do you like to do?"

"Well, you know I've been doing football stats for a long time. I could major in statistics."

"Yes, but honestly, you'd probably have to get a Master's or Doctorate and teach with that kind of degree. What about accounting?" Dad inquired.

"I like numbers, but there's so many rules. My friend showed me his stack of accounting standards books and it doesn't look like much fun to me."

"What about being a doctor, Steve? You seemed to really like that biology class last year. We can figure out the money part of it if you want to go to medical school."

"It was just one class, Mom. I'm really not interested in being a doctor," I retorted, letting the air out of the room. "I could reconsider journalism, though!"

"That's a rough life, Steve. Long hours and weekends, and the pay is not that great. I'd hate for you to have the struggles we've had," Dad shared. "What about finance and banking?"

"It's hard to say. I've only taken one class in finance so far. I'm not exactly dreaming of working in a bank. What if I don't like it?"

"It's a very marketable degree. Bankers and investors make lots of money. It makes sense, Steve," Dad summarized.

And, thus, my major was determined. A lot of pressure had been placed on me to select a major with less than complete information. My parents' logic seemed reasonable and I didn't yet appreciate the importance of such a decision. Thus, with my parents' strong guidance, I moved forward to do my best in my finance concentration.

During my freshman year I had worked at the campus biology lab. It was not as glamorous as it may sound. I basically topped-off thousands of specimen jars of dead animal parts with formaldehyde. Apparently, my high school experience at the burial garment company somehow was viewed as beneficial background. If I wasn't building bridges for a finance career, I was at least building an exceptional résumé to be a zombie caretaker!

Later, I secured a Resident Assistant (RA) role for my sophomore year. It was the first time to truly find my voice. I discovered something I was really good at, both with the residents on my floor and within the RA community. Respect from new freshmen residents was somewhat easy, as they were glassy-eyed and overwhelmed when they arrived on campus. I was accessible on the floor and hosted some introductory meetings and socials, thus embracing this new leadership and mentoring role.

Being a Resident Assistant also provided a small community of fellow RAs to hang out with through the years. But more than that, I found a cause. While the RA job was rewarding in many ways, compensation was slim for the everyday duties and was not fair and equitable considering resident populations, responsibilities, and room size variations amongst the dozens of RAs on campus. By my junior year I rallied RAs together to form the RA Advisory Board to bring a voice to the community and a means to discuss improvements with the university's housing staff. I was the union leader, if you will. We achieved stronger coordination with staff and, more importantly a fair, customized compensation package. This experience highlighted my budding leadership skills.

As my grades reflected my strong study habits, I was inducted into the Golden Key National Honor Society my junior year. I was grateful for such recognition and latched onto the opportunity to extend myself and lead. I volunteered to coordinate Golden Key's regional convention, which brought hundreds to Tuscaloosa my senior winter. Tasks involved coordinating our local team, preparing speakers and luncheons, and engaging with other southern chapters that attended. My superior organizational skills helped support a successful convention.

I'd say my college drinking skills were also superior to that of most of my friends. I took care of my homework and campus jobs by 10 PM, freeing me up for plenty of partying every weekend and some weeknights, too. My casual beer drinking in high school had advanced to more potent drinks with occasional blackouts and mind-rattling hangovers in college. I was very fortunate not to have a car at Alabama. I was severely lacking the self-control to avoid the risks of drunk driving that had already plagued me in high school.

My social life at Alabama continued to revolve around the dorm, our staff, and some of the students on the floor whom I welcomed to frequent weekend trash can hunch punch parties in my spacious, cinder-block private room. Perhaps I abused my position in order to prop up my social life. I stirred up concoctions of vodka (later devolving to pure grain alcohol) with fruit juice, which made it easy to guzzle throughout the night. Sort of like Hi-C gone awry. This usually resulted in a quick buzz, and later a slow walk to the campus strip lined with bars and fast food dives. This was a prime destination for students searching for an early morning snack of pan pizza or Wings & Things with fries and chicken wings gushing grease with every comatose bite. These late-night runs became a habit which, in combination with my drinking, managed to stack the weight on my already husky body.

One such escapade is ingrained in my memory.

After a night of dorm floor revelry, my friend Robert and I ventured out for the evening. On our way back, adequately hydrated and feeling adventurous, we found ourselves in front of the university president's mansion. Though I'd never stolen anything in my life, I was determined to secure a memento of our night, and my hunch punch created just the catalyst. We slithered to the backyard and set our sights on a dimly lit olive-green lantern bolted to the side of a backhouse, which had served as slave quarters in the mid-19th century. After a bit of adrenalin-sponsored twisting and pulling, the lantern sprung free and we began to run through the backyard's overgrown brush to freedom.

Robert led the way and I followed, clutching the lantern to my side. However, in the darkness, I managed to run directly into a sprinkler head about two feet high. It caught me off guard and ripped into my left leg, bringing me down to the ground. I yelled to Robert, "I've been hit!" Robert came back to help me up, and we continued our escape, laughing and limping all the way back to the dorm. I nursed the five-inch scar and kept the unpolished lantern, both mementos of a college night of libation and pilfering.

Perhaps the pinnacle of my college social life was the after party from the Golden Key Regional Convention in February 1988. After leading a successful conference, about a dozen of the delegates caravanned with me to Birmingham to crash my parent's home while they were out of town. Most everyone drank to exhaustion that night.

I paired up with a Georgia co-ed for some mischief in a most odd place. Frolicking on my parents' bed presented a thunderous clash of my college life with my high school home, which proved both thrilling and disturbing. I had sought to keep them separate throughout my four years at Alabama, as evidenced by my infrequent weekends home and my determination to secure campus work each summer. Nevertheless, the next morning we were all able to clean up the house before heading back to Tuscaloosa. Similar to my RA experience, this was another opportunity to leverage my leadership position to indulge in my penchant for drinking. The resultant boost to my self-esteem far outweighed any consideration that I might be abusing my role or leadership position. Furthermore, to my knowledge, my folks never became aware of the college students passed out throughout their house that Saturday evening, or the empty liquor decanters that remained on the bar shelves for years.

My conscientious schoolwork generated a level of stress that was suitably calmed by my drinking and overeating. It happened to be a good match that paid dividends as I prepared to graduate magna cum laude. However, my focus and diligence did not extend from grades to consideration of my future endeavors. Perhaps my lack of passion for careers in finance was now exposing my poor rationale for picking this major in the first place. Now it was nearing time to graduate and enter the real world, but I had neither a clue about my options nor a special drive for any particular path.

I didn't really consider next steps until late February, just a few months prior to graduation. I woke from my senioritis slumber to cobble together a résumé and introduced myself to the university's career planning and placement office. "You are a bit late to get started," the monotone, sweater-clad counselor snipped. "Take a look at the calendar of companies coming to interview and drop your résumé in their folder," was the instruction.

Seemed easy enough, right? But what did I really want to do? I stood in front of the calendar staring, struggling to pull four years of college together to carve a career plan in just moments. I bemoaned seeing my dad struggle in jobs he did not like and was determined not to fall into that same trap, straight out of college. My senior year had sparked my entrepreneurial and leadership ambitions, but through what path? Banking, personal finance advisor, corporate finance? Nothing sounded exciting.

More than anything, I wanted to see more of the world beyond the state of Alabama. After what seemed like hours pondering my future, I relented and dropped my résumé in the North Carolina National Bank (NCNB) envelope. Resigning myself, banking fit my major and Charlotte, North Carolina fit my geographic goal. Yet I was disappointed in my aimless and stale career journey at Alabama. I scanned the list and saw a management training role for Payless Shoe Source. Hmmm, the next Al Bundy from *Married with Children*! Nothing to lose, drop another résumé. I really saw nothing else on the March calendar but thought it might be good to schedule a trial interview with any company just to get comfortable before NCNB. A week prior was another company I recognized: Shell Oil. So, in went my résumé. I shuffled out of the planning office, suddenly realizing school was nearly over and my forward path was ill defined, leaving me concerned about life after graduation.

A week later I got confirmation of my Shell and Payless meetings but NCNB had declined to interview. Perhaps this was the hand of fate at work? Both discussions went well and while I waited for an indication from Payless, Shell offered to fly me to Houston for further interviews. My hostess, Kitty Engstrom, guided me through a long day of office tours, four sets of group interviews with finance, supply, and human resources managers. She also arranged lunch and dinner hosted by various staff intent on putting me at ease while also testing my social skills. Nervous and ill prepared, I was nevertheless able to put a great face on and Kitty and the team seemed impressed. Given my lack of career planning research, I hadn't realized that exciting paths beyond the traditional finance roles could be available. Shell's focus was on opportunities within their product supply organization, specifically supply chain rather than purely finance. This appealed to me a lot, as did the big corporate feel, sense of job security, and opportunity to tackle a variety of roles at one company. It was an exciting prospect. I returned to Tuscaloosa to wait.

Two agonizing weeks later a call came from my Houston hostess. Shell wanted to offer me a role as supply analyst in Houston starting June 6 at a salary of $24,000. I controlled my excitement and, since my interviews had not focused on a particular job, I inquired what, specifically, a supply analyst would do. "You will analyze supply," was her matter-of-fact response. With such clarity and detail, I instantly accepted.

I called home immediately. "Mom, Shell just offered me a job in Houston!"

"Oh, son, how exciting! What did you say?"

"I accepted," I blurted out giddily.

"How much?" Mom asked sheepishly.

"$24,000!" I exclaimed.

"Oh my God, Steve, $24,000!" she repeated, trailing off as if to ponder that much money. And we both screamed "$24,000!" back and forth. What a great moment to share with Mom.

It might not seem like much money to most, but this was more than what my parents brought home together after over thirty years of hard work. After struggling all their lives to provide, Mom and Dad were ecstatic for me to land a secure role, if not career, at Shell.

CHAPTER 8: TURN AROUND

The day finally arrived in early June 1988. All my belongings were packed up in my new light blue Honda Civic as I hugged my parents, jumped in the car, and slowly pulled away for Houston. Admittedly, I was a bit choked up as I saw my folks crying in my rear-view mirror with my childhood home shrinking in the distance. But most of all I was nervous and excited to move on to my new life. My two-day drive across the pine tree-laden hills of Mississippi through the swamplands of Louisiana provided me with ample introspective time to close my Alabama chapter and build up the anticipation of everything new that lay ahead. After arriving in Houston, I leased an apartment and began my first day at Shell on June 6.

At the Shell new employee orientation, I met other recent Alabama alumni. I quickly became close friends with Jim, Kelly, and Debbie, enjoying our freedom from classes and homework and blowing our newfound beer money like we had won the lottery. We welcomed Texas grad Chris into the fold later that summer of '88. Our shared meals at cheap local dives, weekend partying, and some seemingly innocent flirting created our version of the '90s sitcom *Friends*.

Work at Shell was great in my early days as I learned supply chain. I was a scheduler of crude oil ships from West Africa, the Far East, and Mexico, and later coordinated pipeline and barge movements of gasoline and diesel to our northeastern US terminals. Thankfully, these jobs were not just analyzing supply, as my interview hostess had suggested. Success relied upon a lot of analysis and tracking, helping grow my latent planning skills. I felt humble to be making a difference coordinating these items in my first assignments. Product didn't move without my arranging details, often with several other internal groups along with external suppliers and service providers. The fact that these calls often came on weekends and in the middle of the night was a small sacrifice in building my reputation of dependability and diligence. It was a bit surreal to be on the phone with people around the world and taking first class flights to Mexico City, but I enjoyed the business and the people. I felt like I was in the right place.

I received my second assignment in 1989 working on logistical and commercial projects with Shell's fast-growing offshore producing fields. I was thrilled to help determine how new oil and gas production in the Gulf of Mexico would traverse the ocean floor to deliver product to various onshore locations. However, these presentations exposed my lack of speech-making skills. Like many, public speaking was not my sweet spot. I would always have to go to the bathroom before any big presentation. Like clockwork. I tried speech classes where they asked me to expound on a nebulous topic like the rainforest while picturing my audience naked, both of which frankly gave me feelings of apprehension and nausea. I can't say I ever conquered this fear, but over time I leaned on my college habit of intense preparation and my newfound PowerPoint skills to create and share effective presentations.

Meanwhile, the beer junkets with my group of friends helped me wind down from the high demands of work and the pursuit of my career aspirations. We hit the cheap weekday happy hours and checked out the Washington and Westheimer bar scenes on weekends. It was an exhilarating lifestyle, though my curse of drinking and driving returned to my life like an old, comfortable habit. I typically offered to drive, perhaps to avoid the risk of plans being cancelled and my liberating drinking binge being put on hold, or maybe it was a way to boost my ego as a critical part of the group.

In the spring of 1989, we all road-tripped to my favorite party city, New Orleans. Our Houston contingency met up with more friends from Tuscaloosa for the city's annual Jazz Fest party. Given our very limited budget, all ten of us crashed in one room at the Sheraton on Canal Street. We didn't plan to spend much time in the room anyway. The sprawling New Orleans Fairgrounds offered great jazz at nearly a dozen stages, sprinkled with booths to buy beer, gumbo, and barbeque alligator baguettes. We roamed around all day before reuniting with Chris, who had passed out hours earlier behind a huge blown up Bud Light balloon. We caught the last shuttle back to the hotel and then headed to the French Quarter to tour my beloved dives.

We stopped at Pat O'Brien's for drinks and piano bar singing to old reliables like "Sweet Caroline," "Brown-Eyed Girl," and of course, "Piano Man." Through several visits during college, Pat O's exuded a familial draw. We joined hundreds of drunken twenty-somethings singing together while draining several tall glasses of deceivingly tasty fruity Hurricanes. After many hours we moved around the corner, hitting the Dungeon, a nearly pitch-black bar comprised of a few small rooms offering glow-in-the-dark drinks and only classic rock 'n' roll. The Dungeon opened at midnight and closed only after the last patron slinked out past the crack of dawn. That evening we decided to call it a night around 3 AM. On the way back to the hotel I needed to use a restroom, so I made a quick stop at a bar. As is customary, the bar insisted I buy a drink as their toll. By the time I'd finished, my friends had taken off. No worries as I turned right, expecting I wasn't far behind them.

Drunk and tired and expecting to crash in the room in minutes, I never realized I had turned the wrong way out of the bar and had stumbled for likely an hour into the worst part of New Orleans. Suddenly, I was accosted by a faceless thug who shoved a gun at the tip of my nose and demanded my money. Unrattled thanks to my condition, I grabbed my cash and offered it up. Fortunately, my host seemed satisfied and disappeared into the dark. I looked up, bewildered and confused at what just happened and wondering where I should go next. Across the road, just after four o'clock in the morning, I saw an old African-American gray-haired lady gently rocking on her porch. She was staring right at me and motioned as she mumbled, "turn around." I followed her instructions and finally staggered into our hotel room past 5 AM. As a young invincible, I was more proud of my escapade than frightened at the traumatic potential of the moment. I waded through the passed-out bodies and slid into an empty space on the carpet to complete my day.

Back in Houston, occasionally I joined the four-hour weekend traffic jam to Dallas to see Renee and, less often, flew home to Birmingham to see my folks. I tried to convince myself my infrequent visits home were due to my budget and busy lifestyle, but I was just avoiding reminders of the stresses of my teen years and the financial and mental struggles my parents still endured. It wasn't a healthy, supportive way to cope with such situations, but it was an instinctive, subconscious tactic that placed my guilt at the far reaches of my mind.

As the spring of 1989 wore on, I continued to enjoy the social time with friends. Chris and I even jumped in to back up a local pub band's rendition of David Allen Coe's "London Homesick Blues,"which was more a barometer of my drinking skills than my singing or social talents.

It was on one such night that I was chauffeuring the group

home when flashing blue and red lights appeared in my rearview mirror, signaling yet another turning point in my life. Five years since my first DUI in Mountain Brook, I was suddenly reminded of the risks and consequences of my self-medicating lifestyle.

"Touch your nose!"

I shook.

"Walk on this straight line!"

I stumbled.

It was a steamy, dark night at 2 AM on Sunday, June 25, 1989. I stood crooked against my car, with my four friends and drinking partners wedged inside. Somehow, even on this night, I was elected to be the soberest of the bunch. Through the haze of intoxication, I could see my friends peering out the back window to catch a glimpse of the interrogation.

"Where did you go tonight? Did you know you were swerving across the yellow line? Have you had anything to drink?"

How *did* I get to that place in Hunter's Creek Village on the west side of Houston? I couldn't remember.

"Why are you driving? Do you know you could have killed somebody?"

That last question sobered me up quickly. Had I hit anyone? I shot a glance at my car to see if we were still on the road or if we'd been in an accident. The surreal, bleary state was becoming very real, and the fog was clearing. My life had changed in an instant.

I was bombarded with more questions as my mind wandered from stark reality to sluggish exhaustion: "Is this your car? How much did you drink tonight? Have you had any other drugs? Is this the first time you've driven drunk?"

I tried to answer the questions, though I sensed my fate was sealed. The last question pierced me: "Is this the first time you've driven drunk?"

Dad was not there to bail me out. I could imagine the disappointment that would be etched on his face again.

He could never know.

This time I was an adult. There were others in the car. I was not in the warm village of my youth. This was different. Five years later, it would not be so easy.

After being patted down leaning against my car and then cuffed, I was hauled into the Hunter's Creek Village jail about 3 AM. There I answered more questions and was led to my one-person cell like, well, a common criminal. The cell was cold cinder block with a cot and a steel toilet. I sat on the bed and stared at my reflection in the toilet with so much racing through my head. My thinking was still cloudy. I was tired. I was alone. I suspected I had a long road back.

An hour later, after I had dozed off, I heard: "Friedman, let's go!" Two officers decked in their black uniforms opened my cell door and cuffed me again. Where was I going? Could I go home? Were they taking me to my car? No, it wouldn't be that simple. They put me in a squad car to bring me downtown for further processing and holding. This time, I was deposited into a larger cell with benches around the perimeter, another steel toilet (though much filthier), and about a dozen other men. I tried not to stare, but scanned the room to see the homeless vagrants, other likely DUI perpetrators, and a few rough looking thugs, each branded with tattoos and piercings. I was scared.

So many thoughts raced through my head. Why was I driving? What if we had all been injured? What if I had killed someone? Why hadn't I learned anything in the past five years? This wasn't smart. I had to stop. This was my wake-up call. But I knew it wouldn't be so easy. My after-work life revolved around my set of four friends and this is what we did; we went out drinking. How could I just stop that? Things sure had changed from my simple childhood, or was I just grappling with the same issues once again?

After over 12 hours in jail Chris bailed me out. I then spent the rest of my Sunday recovering and then trying to get my thoughts together. I had a court date upcoming. What about fines? Could I lose my license? Would my parents find out? How could this happen? Did I have a drinking problem? Oh my God! Would Shell find out? Could I lose my job?

I couldn't tell anyone at work. I had to make sure Jim and the gang said nothing. Though we didn't work in the same department, I couldn't dare discuss my problem with my drinking friends at work. Others in my office detected my more tense demeanor, but I just brushed it off.

With a sense of both guilt and desperation, I snuck out from work for my court date where I was put on probation with a $750 fine, 30 hours of alcohol treatment counseling, and a cold dose of reality: the next DUI would be jail time and loss of license. I scheduled my counseling for weekends and days off. The sessions mixed dry reminders of the law with suggestions to evaluate my lifestyle and consider Alcoholics Anonymous. It was a lot to absorb. Though I was not prepared to tackle the AA question, I took solace in addressing my troubles as merely excessive social drinking. Still, was this enough for me to be scared straight that summer of 1989?

I was so disappointed in myself. I was building a strong professional reputation at work, yet I was making very poor personal decisions at home.

My friendships drifted apart a bit. Quite natural, I suppose, as the others continued to party together, easily recruiting another willing driver. I was both scared to join in and a bit preachy given the error of my ways, practicing some of my counseling as a means to convert the unconverted— namely myself. Yet, I was also disappointed that my friends hadn't rallied around me to support me through this period. Suddenly, with my social rug pulled out from under me, my sensitive balance of diligent worker by day and partier by night was disrupted. I felt lost and lonely once again.

CHAPTER 9: STRIKING

As noted, my dating experience in high school and college was less than stellar. Hindered by my shyness and low self-esteem, I rarely put myself out there with the ladies. Only in my last semester at Alabama did I start to recognize that some of my leadership positions on the RA Advisory Board and Golden Key seemed to develop a level of bravado that emitted some sort of hormone that select girls picked up on, like a cat in heat. I had more dates in that final semester than my whole life to that point. It was a fun way to end college life and provided cause for optimism for my future dating prospects. But that momentum did not carry over to my first year and a half in Houston. My lone date ended with a cute, very nice girl apparently less than enchanted with my undeveloped kissing skills while on her couch after dinner and a movie. Rather than trying to turn the moment into a learning lab, I slinked out to end the evening. Such an ego destroying moment probably did more to stunt my dating ambitions than even my social anxiety.

However, in January 1990, desperate to re-energize my social life and turn a new leaf from my recent DUI setback, I was determined to reach out. Though I was never very religious, I discovered a singles Shabbat service on Friday nights. I planned to attend the next one on February 2 in pursuit of some new friends, and perhaps new avenues of guidance and support through these lonely and confusing times. I also signed up for a Jewish singles bowling social that Sunday morning at 9 AM. Enough wallowing around.

Services were nothing life changing, though I was glad to put myself out there and boasted to my parents about my modest reconnection with Judaism.

The next night, Jim asked me to pick up my old friends at a bar as no one was in good condition to drive. The irony was not lost on me. However, I chauffeured and returned home for a short night's sleep. Though I'd never been to a Jewish singles' event before, the evening's reminder of my dismal social life got me out of bed on a chilly Sunday morning. Unbeknownst to me, across town an attractive, reserved young lady, Jennifer Snitz, was recovering from hosting a hot tub party with a dozen of her friends. That morning, her dad nagged her to clean up and go to her scheduled bowling social.

Jennifer and I bowled separately but introduced ourselves at the lunch that followed. Sitting next to each other, we struck up a conversation that carried on throughout lunch, as if no one else was around. Jennifer was 21 and a transplant from Kansas City and the University of Missouri. She was taking a break from college and working a temp role as a paralegal while living with her dad, who had recently separated and moved to Houston for a fresh start.

It was obvious I'd met my true and special match on February 4. It was love at first strike! Years later I memorialized the occasion for a birthday celebration:

Love at First Strike!

Some of you may not be aware of how Jennifer and I met,
So, on the eve of her birthday I'll drop some clues you
    might get.

We met on a Sunday morning way too early,
In a somewhat dark yet crowded Houston alley.
She was an old hat at this social dating game,

I was a bit new with my slightly awkward frame.

When the games were over, we met to eat with all,
Prepared to chitchat, kibbutz, and have a ball.

Jenn squeezed in next to me to grab a chair,
No time to waste, no time to spare.

We exchanged casual introductions to one another,
Being careful not to bring the conversation into the
gutter.

We talked to each other as the time went by unaware,
Of the others in the crowd, the time we could not share.

She was so radiant, a face I immediately could adore,
For this seemed to me clearly like a must-score.

I tried not to be too odd or overly quirky,
So, I ordered the fries with a side of turkey.

We talked about family, jobs, and what we like,
I could tell already this was quite a strike!

We exchanged numbers; it was definitely a hit,
Then we said our goodbyes; it was time to split.

As I drove my car home for a happy spin,
I was ecstatic, I felt at this point as if life would begin.

For me there was nothing sad or foul,
I thought of her face and began to howl.

Yes, we met at a bowling alley, yes indeed,
It wasn't long before we were dating at breakneck speed.

We couldn't wait to make our lives together the best,
Always linked back to the alley in Houston Southwest!

We were love-struck. Two rather shy people feeling a
comfortable connection from the start. I was mesmerized by
her, and by the ease of our conversations. Jennifer was kind,

smart, and beautiful. As a shy, anxious, and slightly chubby person, I felt relaxed and warm around her. She shared her life story and dreams with me and listened intently to mine. For the first time, I was the object of someone's focus and care. Though reserved at her core, she was more outgoing than me, which made me feel secure and gave me the courage to reach out more. We started dating immediately and never looked back.

Our first real date was at Uno's Pizzeria, followed by a marathon get-to-know-you session in my car in a grocery parking lot talking about family, background, hopes and wishes until 2 AM. I'm typically not one for small talk and Jennifer was happy to have more substantive, revealing discussions. She did not seem to notice my shortcomings.

Oddly, I didn't feel compelled to don my drinking mask in order to relax with her. It was quite strange. Since even my pre-teens my nerves and concerns had been relieved by alcohol. It became so habitual that I often pre-medicated in college and with my Houston friends before going out into social settings. Yet now, with Jennifer, I had no draw for such an elixir. It's like the instinct had been removed, replaced by a belongingness I barely recognized from my youth. We became quite a pair.

Ten days later we double-dated with Jim and his new girlfriend, Debbie, for Valentine's Day at Dong Ting's Chinese Restaurant. I had bought Jennifer a box of chocolates the night before, but when I came home from work to get the chocolates I found that my bachelor pad ants had beaten me to it. Luckily, my neighbor came to the rescue and offered me her chocolates for my big date. Jennifer says she knew that night that we were going to get married. I think I knew at the bowling alley.

Later in February I invited Jennifer over for our first home-cooked meal. While I'm certainly no culinary expert, I can manage to read directions—or so I thought. Unfortunately, interpreting those directions can be a challenge. Hence, my red pepper-stuffed chicken ended up with a whole spice jar of hot red pepper flakes rather than the diced fresh red bell peppers the recipe intended. It seemed quite odd when I assembled it, but not nearly as weird as it tasted as we nibbled around the edges until the inside of our noses burned and we relegated ourselves to Domino's Pizza.

Jennifer and I had not been dating long when she joined me for a Saturday afternoon at the office so I could catch up on some work and prepare for my presentations the following week. Once we parked the car in the One Shell Plaza garage, we approached the door to the elevator lobby.

"At Shell there is a secret code to enter the building." I placed my hand on the grip. "Three quick turns down," I mumbled as if trying to remember the sequence. "Wait a second, and then one more turn, then two more quick turns." I then proceeded to open the door.

Jennifer looked at me inquisitively but seemed to buy the story until my grinning face gave it away. "You're pulling my leg," she suggested. And thus concluded her introduction to my awkward, if not mildly annoying, sense of humor. Nonetheless, she stuck with me anyway and we both have a chuckle when either of us recreates the combination lock at new doors.

On February 4 my life changed completely. With Jennifer I felt this connection and comfort I had never known before. Though embarrassed, I nervously shared my past troubles with alcohol and my DUI with Jennifer. She listened, consoled, and accepted. She later stated it did not leave "a huge impression" since we'd already gotten to know each other. As a result, I could let go of my caustic social life, which was so entangled around drinking. She declared, "I was a huge reason why you turned your life around," which I have always joyfully acknowledged. Our relationship enabled me to rise from the depths of my loneliness and DUI recovery and bask in a happier and safer lifestyle filled with love.

Less than a month into our new relationship, I made the bold move to ask Jennifer to join some friends and me for our annual Jazz Fest experience in New Orleans in late April. Without hesitation, Jennifer accepted the invitation. We had such a great time enjoying the jazz at the fairgrounds and introducing Jennifer to all my New Orleans favorites, most especially the piano bar of Pat O's. While we had some drinks along the way, neither of us felt compelled to overindulge, happy to be high on the energy between us. It presented a stark contrast to the previous year's drunken adventures at Jazz Fest.

After long days of work, we would often be up until the middle of the night talking, laughing, and dreaming at my apartment until she had to dart home to get some sleep before the next day's work. In the past, if I was up until such late hours, I was usually on the verge of passing out. Though it took a bit of getting used to myself, it was quite a relief to extract that need from my social life, not to mention the temptation to drink and drive. In so many ways, Jennifer was my angel. I believe to my core that she saved me from myself; she saved my life. It wouldn't be the last time.

Meanwhile, wondering what the catch was in our easygoing relationship, we tried to restrain ourselves from moving too fast. We filled each other's need for love, which both of us had struggled to find as adults. We never argued, perhaps because our personalities were so similar—both compromisers by nature who steered away from conflict. Jennifer and I were clearly attracted to each other and by mid-year we were practically living together. I'm sure we both saw this as testing ground for our next step together, but it seemed so natural.

During that summer we made our pilgrimages for family introductions. First we travelled to Kansas City to see Jennifer's beloved grandparents and Aunt Marilyn. We received a warm embrace from Jennifer's extended family. Next we flew to Birmingham for greetings with my parents and sisters. Most everyone embraced us and could sense our loving bond. My mom, however, was a bit reluctant to let her baby go, especially after such a short courting. She pulled me aside to suggest we needed more time, perhaps to test my resolve. This pained me, as I yearned for her approval. My whole childhood revolved around the bond with my mother. Yet, I knew this was my destiny, and I was prepared to move on with Jennifer alone if it ever came to that. I never shared this conversation with Jennifer. She was already overwhelmed by the stress of trying to fit into those early family outings. Another shy person like me trying to get a word in amongst my chatty family was never easy, I know. Mom eventually came around as she observed Jennifer's kindness and my happiness.

Though it had only been six months since we met, by late summer I could tell we were both ready to make it official. I was determined to provide a memorable scene for this momentous occasion. However, after rain cancelled my plans for popping the big question at our favorite talking-place on the rocks of our neighborhood lake, I finally dropped to my knees to express my love and ask for her hand during an August weekend vacation at South Padre Island. Unfortunately, by the time I found the perfect spot (isolated from the typically crowded beach), the sun had set and she couldn't see the ring. After Jennifer cried "yes!" we scurried to find some light for her to see the rock. Once home, we quickly began our plans for a June wedding in Houston.

Our wedding was such a joyous occasion, hosted at Vargo's restaurant on June 23, 1991. We selected this gorgeous lakeside garden scene as we envisioned our outdoor wedding at the grand gazebo with peacocks strutting about. Mom suggested I ask Dad to be my best man and I agreed, never one to disappoint my Mom. Dad and I shared an unspoken bond, given our similar dispositions, yet the relationship still lacked the dialog and guidance I'd needed throughout my youth. However, I had few other candidates beyond the intermittent casual friends from different periods of my life. Mom, meanwhile, had warmed up to her future daughter-in-law and gave Jennifer permission "to slap Stephen around if he gets out of line." When Mom includes you in her humor, you know you've been accepted.

Jennifer's maid of honor was her Aunt Marilyn, whom she was close to throughout her life—especially after Jennifer's mother, Gwendolyn, passed away from cancer at 28, when Jennifer was six. Jennifer had been adopted by her father's new wife and later joined by a new brother and sister, but the loss of her mom left an indelible gap in her life.

Though the scorching Texas heat and threat of rain forced us to move the festivities inside, the dining room lit up when Jennifer stepped into view around the corner. As she approached, I beamed at her breathtaking beauty. After a somewhat frustrating and lonely adolescence, we had found each other. We could both finally exhale, and then radiate, anticipating the life of friendship and love we would have together.

Our traditional Jewish wedding was performed under the *chuppah* or flower-adorned cloth canopy. Jennifer circled me seven times, a Biblical concept denoting perfection or completeness, and then I crushed a glass with a stomp of my right foot signifying that joy must always be tempered to survive. After dinner, the party continued with many toasts from the crowd and dancing until midnight, including the traditional Hora during which we were hoisted up on chairs while the crowd sang and danced in circles around us. The whole evening was an amazing party, surrounded by friends and family. The next week we celebrated our unity with a Bahamas cruise and a few days in Disney World before returning to Houston to formally begin our life together.

I finally gave myself permission to relax and enjoy the moment.

Within this cocoon that I hadn't known since my childhood, I felt warmth, friendship, partnership, love, and relief.

CHAPTER 10: EQUILIBRIUM

The early '90s were literally our honeymoon period. After getting married in the summer of 1991, Jennifer and I enjoyed discovering ourselves, both as a couple and individually. We bonded over late night talks, caught two-for-$1 movies at the theatre, and ate out often. We traveled a bit together, seeing family and grabbing some weekends in Austin, San Antonio, and New Orleans. The more we got to know each other, the closer we became. We enveloped each other like a warm blanket.

Within this comfort, perhaps for the first time, I reflected on who I was, and why. At 25, I was a hard-working individual with an insatiable desire for love and acceptance. Yet I was also a shy guy who did not feel comfortable in social settings, either at work or at play. But it seemed like more than just shyness or discomfort. I had always felt different, like people were watching me under the microscope. My odd social scenes— when I mixed up names, fumbled through stories, and got run over by other more verbose and smoother talkers than me— became the source of wonder, perhaps even laughter, amongst others. I could not get out of the closet that Isaac had put me in nearly 20 years earlier. So, I had chosen to lean on alcohol through my early twenties to dull the apprehension and, in a sense, to remove me from the presence of the situation.

Timid and weak, I had expected finding the love I craved was a long shot, until I met Jennifer. Our relationship helped me to replace drinking with a healthy, supportive relationship. She had rescued me at my low point. But had all my ills been cured?

Shortly after getting married, I attended a Shell leadership course that provided some reflective exercises. Contrary to the extrovert label I'd carried since my journalism camp 10 years earlier, I was assessed as considerably introverted. Though I had always suspected the previous label was unfitting, it enabled me to take a degree of comfort that I appeared to align with societal norms. Maybe the tag could have emboldened me over the past decade, but instead it largely made me feel like a failure, unable to live up to the branding I'd been given. Sure, I'd made friends at college and upon arrival in Houston, but these relationships were typically propped up by alcohol. I still felt exhausted from the mental exertion. The re-labeling thus didn't come as a big shock, but it flipped the tables on my perspective.

In the Shell class, I learned that introversion was often confused with shyness, both of which could result in low self-esteem. While people could perhaps relate more to one of these traits than the other, they often can be intertwined.

Shyness reflected my fear of social settings and interactions, often as a result of rough conversational skills. I felt shy since I was a youngster. Often, I forgot people's names as soon as they were spoken, due to my heightened sense of anxiety. I've always felt inadequate as the center of attention, whether in the simplest scenes such as going around a meeting room for introductions and icebreakers, or in the most challenging situations like cocktail gatherings with a room of strangers. Small talk was never my forte. Thinking of what to say and forming an interesting discussion on the fly was overwhelming. Extracting myself from those conversations was almost as difficult as trying to insert myself into a discussion in the first place.

Introversion, on the other hand, related to my motivations and how I got energy. Everyone needs to recharge batteries. I've always preferred time alone or with family. I typically recuperated by myself. Some of my favorite times were reading books or running errands, grabbing lunch, or catching a movie alone.

Many feed off social energy and feel most lively when conversing at gatherings. They would find my solitude uncomfortable and lonely. While I had discovered that some may be shy and others introverted, I was undeniably both. It was no wonder I took comfort in my earlier "extrovert" label when I found the thesaurus offered synonyms for extroverts like "socializers, livewires, gregarious people, befrienders," while introverts were "recluses, hermits, loners, shrinking violet[s]." Though only 60% of Americans fit the label, extroverts often make the best first impressions that win over crowds in social situations and at work meetings through their command of the room, gift of gab, and high degree of self-confidence.

Despite learning more about my shyness and introversion, I was ill equipped to find peace with either trait. Thus, I was tormented by my own perception that I was a second-class citizen, a feeling I had already worn for decades.

This introspection made me keenly aware of the risks of becoming depressed and even reclusive if I obsessed about such shortcomings. So I opted to stay at the surface, taking away some recognition of my strengths and discomforts but avoiding a journey to truly come to grips with my demons. Thus, I remained handicapped when engaging with most others.

Jennifer also had a shy and introverted streak, though she was drawn more toward building friendships than me. With Jennifer by my side, we were determined to at least make small steps toward socializing. One such social opportunity presented itself after we settled into our first apartment. We sought to expand our circle with Bob and Mindy, acquaintances of Jennifer's. We boldly invited them over, had nice conversation over dinner, and popped a Blockbuster movie into our VCR. The conversation was engaging, but perhaps the exhaustion from the week or our need to recharge kicked in just a little too early. Midway through the movie both Jennifer and I dozed off while lying on the floor together that Friday night. We awoke to the clicking sound as the tape completed its automatic rewind. We then discovered our guests had gone. We never caught up with them again. Perhaps they were put off by our lack of hosting skills, or maybe they just didn't like our movie selection.

But introversion went beyond the social scene. At work, one of my early bosses coached me on being too aloof: "Slow down. Chitchat more." While I was indeed quiet on the surface, given my reserved and nervous nature, I was also busy in my head which I then tracked with intricate spreadsheets for projects, work tasks, staff evaluations, goals, and family vacations.

Far removed from my fly-by-night college days, I now relied on a meticulous calendar of meetings and task to-do lists ever since Jennifer graced me with my first Franklin Planner in the early '90s. One co-worker observed my detailed planning and offered: "You are *addicted* to that Franklin!" The word "addicted" rang in my head as I reflected on my drinking, overeating, gambling, and now planning. My life was a string of addictive behaviors that provided self-preservation for my fragile ego.

This latest rendition of extreme planning and preparation was no different. The resultant positions conveyed in a calm and methodical way could be quite impactful once others recognized their value. I was now acutely focused on going beyond the expectations of the job in order to contribute more and be noticed without being verbose or flashy. I discovered new tactics for managing seasonal product requirements in the Northeast and optimized barge capacity throughout our system. I tackled these goals with the vigor of an obsessed taskmaster.

While I needed to prepare, extroverts on the other hand tended to think quickly, responding off the cuff. To see such people at work jumping in with facts and figures, comfortably debating topics on the fly, was quite impressive and intimidating. I think introverts such as myself must be in it for the long haul. But in a world dominated by verbose conversationalists, it was always hard for me to get a word in much less get recognized. The world seemed to move at a much faster pace.

As with my other addictive behaviors, this compulsion occasionally got out of control either at work or at home. When Jennifer and I bought our first house in 1992, we quickly envisioned many HGTV-inspired projects. Once moved in, we began our various home projects: installing kitchen backsplash, wallpapering the front reading room, building a storage hut, and plotting our grand backyard landscaping vision with boxes of pencils and yards of string.

The first part of our backyard adventure involved tearing out the grass on the side of the house and scattering a gallon of wildflower seeds and some steppingstones around a lovely birdbath. After a few weeks the flowers sprouted, and it presented eye-popping bright yellows, flaming reds, and coarse greens. Only a few weeks later we realized these flowers-in-a-box don't stop growing. Soon, they were knee-high and then waist-high weeds! The beautiful picture on the cannister turned into a scene from *Honey I Shrunk the Kids!* If only my compulsion to plan and tackle projects was matched by my handyman skills.

Meanwhile, my compulsive determination at work managed to push me out of my comfort zone, masking my inhibitions. This wasn't going to convert me into a gregarious socialite, but it did help me find a new equilibrium without drinking. Rather than slide into a reclusive, comfortable place of solitude, I pushed myself out into the world in order to meet my own high expectations. This seemed like a healthy balance, though it proved very hard to maintain.

As I had learned, an introvert's creative inner sanctum stereotypically leans toward roles in the arts (painting, writing, poetry), numbers (accounting, statistics), or analysis (economists, strategists), more so than roles reliant upon frequent social interactions and quick processing (salespeople, marketers, negotiators, lawyers, and politicians). My jobs in those early years were more logistical and operational—a perfect match for my personality.

In subsequent roles, I was creating a lot of charts and slides, plotting logistical options and economics for new offshore Gulf of Mexico oil platforms, and spending a lot of time scheduling or coordinating crude oil and product movements. I was very busy as the "hub of the wheel," as one of my later staff put it, working with the commercial staff and with terminal operators to ensure product arrived at the right place, right time, and right cost. My strengths fit most job tasks well, though my conversations were more transactional then relationship-based. No wonder my current analytical job was so reassuring. It all seemed to make sense. Hence, work at Shell was generally satisfying and rewarding.

My passion and skills shone through via numerous recognition awards and promotions. Perhaps these acknowledgments were more hard-fought as an introvert who tended to fly under the radar. Nevertheless, just as with my RA and Golden Key recognition in college, a nice pat on the back went a long way. Any bonuses were certainly welcome, but honestly it was the ego boosts that assured me I was doing a good job and was appreciated.

Occasionally I reflected on my past drinking habit. I realized that I had used those same analytical skills to scrutinize my actions during my years of drinking. Clearly, I knew and experienced some of the repercussions of excessive drinking during that period. However, I must have subconsciously determined the salvation of my drinking far outweighed the risks. For the first time, my introspective approach helped me better understand myself.

Thus, the loving relationship at home and the satisfying contributions at work combined to provide a happy period for me after spending previous years wondering if I would ever find love and if I would excel in the business environment. To satisfy those unknowns was liberating.

After nearly a year trying to grow our family, in 1993 we finally got pregnant with our first child and our next chapter was about to begin. In the meantime, Jennifer and I decided to explore relocation. Armed with a new night school MBA, I discussed with my manager my interest to work in the field, to see the country, and to get more hands-on leadership experience. My manager indicated he needed some time to research options and would get back to me soon. In the meantime, Jennifer and I scanned the Shell Distribution map to envision life in exciting faraway places like California, Virginia, Boston, or perhaps Chicago.

Ultimately, with many home projects in mid-stream, I was offered a transfer to a great supervisory opportunity in Detroit, Michigan. I hired a contractor who finished our inside projects, and Jennifer and I boxed up our pencils and string and headed to the Motor City.

CHAPTER 11: THE STUDENT

Detroit was an interesting place to be. It didn't have the amazing scenery of California or the history of New England or the ambience of Chicagoland, but Detroit offered a serene suburban home for us to settle down and grow our family. It also provided a tremendous leadership testing ground for me as part of an informal rotation plan that brought young professionals through Detroit every two years.

Fortunately, Shell avoided introducing Jennifer and me immediately to the brutally cold weather of the Great Lakes by cleverly transferring us up in May of 1994. Spring had sprung; flowers of all colors were blooming amidst a plush carpet of thick bright green grass, and the mild temperatures were a welcome reprieve from the brutal Houston climate—especially given that Jennifer was five months pregnant when we arrived. The suburbs were reminiscent of Mayberry-type small towns and villages connected by rolling hills. The beautiful and soothing landscape reminded me of the tranquility of Mountain Brook and Jennifer of the warmth of her Overland Park, Kansas upbringing.

With the baby due in four months, our arrival offered ample time to acclimate to our surroundings, select new doctors, and prepare our lives for our new family. In searching for a new obstetrician, Jennifer was provided with a lead by my new co-worker's wife who scribbled down her doctor's details on a napkin. Later, Jennifer deciphered the note as Dr. Hutton O'Boin. I thought it sounded fine—a nice Irish guy. However, after trying to schedule our first appointment, we discovered his name was actually Dr. Hutton, and his specialty OBGYN. Ends up he would play a less prominent role than expected.

As our mild, breezy summer gave way to a cooling fall, the baby's kicks and punches became mild cramps the evening of September 12. Having heard the forewarnings that early contractions may be false and that first deliveries could provide arduous waiting periods made all the more uncomfortable by the sterile atmosphere of a hospital room, we relaxed around our apartment. Jennifer called her mom, we went for a late night walk, and then Jennifer took a warm shower until finally, at 3 o'clock in the morning, she declared it was time to head to the hospital.

From that point, it was like a dam had ruptured. Water was literally breaking. Screams were coming from the passenger seat. Thoughts of delivering in the car flashed through my head. Pleadings to drive faster gave way to threats of bodily injury if I stopped at one more light. Finally, our 30-minute sprint landed us at William Beaumont Hospital's emergency entrance. As we squealed to a stop, the attendants pulled Jennifer into a wheelchair and I was left to park the car.

I sprinted to the lobby, scribbled my signature through five agonizing minutes of paperwork, and dashed to the room to find Jennifer parked on the bed. I stood by her side, rattled a bit by the speed of events. Jennifer was in full labor. In her desperation, she now opted to muffle her own screams and pain by attempting to bite off my right thumb. I snapped it back and reminded her of our Lamaze training, but only received a searing glance. I asked if she wanted an epidural, but the nurse insisted that Jennifer was too far along. Finally, the nurse relented to her pleadings to push. She forewarned of 30 minutes of suffering ahead before Dr. Hutton would arrive to deliver. Meanwhile, the nurse scooted to the other side of the room to straighten some spare linens. Jennifer squeezed my hand and bore down with a grunting push. As I looked down in amazement, I impulsively blurted: "There sure is a lot of hair on that head!"

The room filled with conflicting sounds: Baby Gwen's first gasping cries, Jennifer's shrills of pain and relief, and finally the nurse's shriek pierced the room. "STOP PUSHING!" she yelled as she darted to the foot of the bed to catch our new baby. Moments later, the room became a harmony of sighs and coos, relief that the big event was over. A new baby scent blended with the musty odors of sweat soaked into the many folds of the off-white sheets, under which lay Jennifer, the world's newest mom. She was exhausted but anxious to see Gwendolyn.

The attendant pushed me over to a small table with a hot yellow light beaming onto our baby. It was my turn to sever the cord that had been her lifeline for nearly nine months. My eyes darted from Gwen's bright pink, pudgy face to the small pre-school-like scissors shaking in my hand. I pushed down as they cut through the cord, setting Gwendolyn free. My mind was swirling at the quick birth and blitz of activity. The nurse finally laid Gwen into her first blanket, adorned with light blue and pink stripes on opposite ends, and passed Gwen to her mommy. Jennifer reached out to hold her baby for the first time. Exhausted, but running on adrenalin as she stared into Gwen's eyes, her smile faded. "She has Down syndrome."

Though prenatal testing had not indicated a particular risk, Jennifer did have some premonitions after watching a documentary about a son with Down syndrome and sighting a couple of young kids with Down syndrome in the weeks leading up to our dash to the hospital. I had discounted such thoughts as paranoia and had expected a "normal" baby. In the hospital, our exhaustion blended with tears, which then gave way to guilt. Was this our fault? Something we did in the past nine months? Something in her genes or mine? The thoughts we'd shared throughout the pregnancy of our new baby going to school, riding a bike, graduating, falling in love, having kids all flashed before us with sadness and angst. All these plans had changed. What if she couldn't do any of this? We were drowning in grief. Scared and overwhelmed, we could hardly stay afloat.

In the days and weeks that followed, we shrugged off our tears and worries and immersed ourselves into the special needs community to understand more about Gwen and her fate. While we were assured she could grow to be a strong, capable, loving adult, we were overwhelmed with the school-aged challenges that many of the parents were drowning in.

We quickly retracted from the groups to focus on just hugging and loving on our new baby—all four pounds, two ounces of her. She was so beautiful. Her bright blue eyes, her cooing, and her tiny toes. She had the calmest demeanor. We took her everywhere, like a suitcase. She would sleep through our dinner and movie date nights like a champion. But she also would struggle to stay awake to take her bottle, due to her low muscle tone and sedentary manner. By the time she took her prescribed amount, we only had an hour before we needed to wake up and repeat the task. Typical of first-time parents, we meticulously recorded her feedings and diaper duties to take comfort in her progress. Other than her diagnosis, she was healthy, avoiding many of the heart, digestive tract, or cranial complications that can often accompany Down syndrome.

We soon began to share Gwendolyn with the world. We introduced her to family, co-workers, and friends to a mixture of excitement from some, comfort from others, and trepidation from the rest. Many just didn't know how to react, or provided frivolous but well-meaning comments like "God only gives you what you can handle," or "Gwen picked you because you are special people." We eventually tuned out the world around us and the loads of information and books we had gathered and just embraced the amazement of Gwen's every sound and movement and our lives became filled with joy.

In the meantime, after the leaves changed colors to yellow and rust, some light snow dusted the grass in October. Autumn finally gave way to piles of snow and bone-chilling negative temperatures by the end of the year. The white snow became stacked dark gray heaps, and the roads became ice skating rinks. But, unlike Birmingham, this was not an overnight disappearing act and would prove to be a solid six months in the icebox, eventually giving way to a spring thaw only when late April crept around.

In the depths of winter, we decide to try for another baby. It had taken us over a year to get pregnant with Gwen, and our doctors suggested it would be good for her to have a role model. In January, we learned we were pregnant once again. We did opt to have extensive genetic testing done, more so to prepare ourselves rather than toward ending any less-than-perfect forecast. Nevertheless, we did feel some guilt-ridden relief when all tests returned normal.

We were both excited to be pregnant once again. I use the misplaced "we," since I did contribute to the condition at hand, though I certainly claim no part in the sweats, cravings, nausea, or weakness. I did manage to gain 20 pounds with each of our babies. However, I didn't have the good fortune of passing most of that in one monstrous grunt and push. So I joined Jennifer in shopping for larger sized clothes. Our growing family offered Jennifer perfect inroads into the active new moms' groups of the suburbs and her calendar became quite busy with play dates and maternity store shopping.

Early contractions left Jennifer bed-ridden for the last couple of months of her pregnancy, and I slid to the night shift at the plant to help care for Gwen during the day. Finally, less than a year and a half since coming to Detroit, Madolyn Raye arrived on the scene to remind us that calm and sleepy babies are not the norm. Nevertheless, we beamed at our girls every time we wrapped them up in coats, scarves, mittens, hats, and boots for those blistering Detroit winters.

Contrary to the homey suburbs, Detroit's inner city was fraught with crime and racial divide, struggling to recover from a sluggish economy spurred on by the Big Three automakers' pullback. Unemployment, poverty, and tensions so enraged the downtrodden that they set their own neighborhoods on fire, most especially the night before Halloween, which the city ominously labeled "Devil's Night." The once majestic home of Ford's Model T and the Motown Sound was now a sad, if not scary, place.

My work home, the Shell Distribution Terminal, was in one such neighborhood: River Rouge. The first week of my commute I drove by a chalk outline of a body from the battles the night before, and just a few mornings later I passed by a smoldering car fire from the previous evening's warfare—a mere block from our gasoline depot. It was a bit scary, and underscored my shift from the corporate tower I'd worked in up to that point.

Working at the terminal was an eye opening learning experience. The terminal included about 30 employees – a manager and three supervisory staff including myself, five operators responsible for maintaining the facility's tanks, pipes, and truck loading equipment, and 20 drivers who rotated 24/7 to deliver product to the network of Shell gas stations in and around Detroit. I was the newest supervisor at the plant, scheduled to rotate from operations to delivery, and later to oversee a few smaller satellite terminals in Michigan and Ohio. Throughout the industry, terminals were struggling due to inefficient operations and costly overhead. Rumors of consolidation and outsourcing had been swirling around Detroit and other big terminals for years. Freshly equipped with my MBA, I felt empowered to bring my leadership know-how to help reverse Shell Detroit's fortunes.

Our plant was unionized, as one might expect in Detroit. I would certainly gain the leadership experience that I sought after my MBA. Cutting my supervisory teeth at such an early stage in my career was likely to distinguish me from others as I set my sights on management positions down the road.

However, I quickly realized I was not to be the teacher, but the student. This plant had tested many young transferees before me, and they would have many opportunities to show me the ropes. My analytical approach of tabulating delivery time and posting inefficiency scores was not well received. My discomfort with conflict was a glaring gap when trying to preach safety and efficiency to ornery old stalwarts, some of whom had been at the terminal longer than I'd been on this planet. Going toe-to-toe was not fun for me, nor was it my strength. I shied away to avoid offending others. I lacked the confidence to debate and defend my positions, and the courage to admit my deficiencies and ask questions to learn.

Nevertheless, I was keenly aware of my leadership role and thus began to force myself into precarious situations if I felt safety or proper staff coaching was necessary. In Detroit I learned a lot about relating to people and the quiet leadership of "show, don't tell." Over time, I rode on many rides with the drivers, both day and night. I came down to the terminal in the middle of the evening when operational issues arose, such as unexpected plant shutdowns due to mechanical problems. As I relaxed my rigid approach, my reserved nature slowly gave way to relationship building and patience. Gradually, we made some progress in improving the culture and delivery of the terminal.

Given the very different backgrounds of the terminal staff and the long commutes back to the peacefulness of our suburban families, we rarely socialized outside of work hours. The strong undertones of operational and driver safety within Shell's distribution organization ensured that drinking and driving was never an option. We had little time for weekend socializing or traveling, given our busy homefront. We didn't even journey across the bridge to Sarnia, on the Canadian side of the river, until our tenure was nearly complete. Yet we bonded together as a family and after two years we prepared for our return to Houston.

Unfortunately, five years after my departure from Detroit, under the weight of many of the challenges I sought to rectify, Shell closed the plant, folding into Amoco's terminal up the street and replacing Shell drivers with contractors.

SECTION THREE - CHAOS

CHAPTER 12: FAKE YOU!

In the spring of 1996, our two year "leadership training/ baby factory" adventure concluded. Jennifer was sorry to say goodbye to friends and the beautiful landscapes, but we were both happy to avoid a third blustery winter. Additionally, the added cost of two babies and a second car in Detroit had drained our bank account. We were ashamedly charging groceries and timing our checks. Our return to Houston enabled us to get back on our feet. Jennifer's dad graciously offered to move out of his own house and provided his home to us for free. We sold one car upon our return and I relegated myself to long bus commutes downtown.

A role had been created back in the same supply department where I'd scheduled products before leaving for Detroit, but now I would be trading distillates (diesel and jet fuel). Basically, I was buying and selling product to supply Shell's retail requirements in order to fulfill our customer demand at airports and Shell service stations. I was excited to return to an organization with so many friendly faces. With my strong scheduling background in supply and new supervisory experience, it seemed like a natural progression from an operational to commercial role with greater impact on the bottom line.

I immediately dug into the details including product specifications, typical volumes to buy and sell each month by location, and pricing options. However, what I soon realized was the role leaned considerably on external stakeholder management and the social demands of building such relationships. I would be working with many other energy companies to negotiate purchases and sales. There was no way to avoid these anxiety-riddled interactions. It was core to the job. As I found in Detroit with staff engagements, I expected such adjustments would take time and energy.

I was falling into a corporate conundrum so many people battle. The greatest perceived value for the company was derived from deal-making (sales, negotiations, and trading) and the very extroverted skills of thinking on one's feet and socializing. I discovered that in Shell's supply department, it was an unwritten expectation that one's career path started with analysis, wove through some scheduling roles, and then escalated to commercial trading jobs before opening up management possibilities. For those who didn't want that progression or couldn't prove their abilities, their career path was often stunted. They either stalled out or left Shell to define a different path.

My success through eight years at Shell had provided a degree of confidence. So, while it seemed like a natural progression from analytical and operational roles for me, my career path was luring me out of my comfort zone and into a life filled with excitement and challenge—and considerable stress.

The security I craved told me I needed to stay at Shell. The need to provide for my growing family fed my compulsion to work hard and disregard any apprehension. Besides, maybe the transition to a more social role wasn't as daunting as I'd made it out to be in my head? Thus, my trait of pursuing stretch goals, even without consideration of the fit or personal cost, actually gave me the conviction to attack this new challenge head on.

I was committed to make the necessary connections. However, I found my attempts a bit clunky. It was hard to drum up casual chitchat with trading partners on the phone.

So just a month into the job, I signed up for an industry golf scramble. Nearly everyone in the department played golf. I had never tried golf beyond the occasional round of windmill-laden sloping putt-putt courses. So, I took a few lessons at a local driving range and flew to Cleveland to introduce myself to the industry at BP's annual golf scramble. Unfortunately, I was placed on a team determined to take home the trophy. I hated to disappoint them, but I was horrible. My swings missed the ball more than they hit that dimpled devil. My lone feeble attempt at industry golfing was embarrassing and I swore off the game rather than dedicate hours away from family to try to reach a presentable threshold. I was fine to leave this frustration behind, but I sacrificed a good chance to fit in with the trading community.

Meanwhile, my trading territory was initially coast-to-coast, which necessitated covering four time zones each day. My trading schedule and meticulous style were not always most efficient, thus necessitating even longer hours in the office—including some weekends—just to organize my desk and plan for the week ahead.

Jennifer was happy to be back in Houston. She recognized the big leap I was making at work and the time commitment involved. As always, she was quite supportive. But raising two girls just 13 months apart was becoming a handful. Days were filled with play dates, appointments, housework, and nurturing time with the girls. Both began walking about the same time. By the age of two, Madolyn began to pass up Gwen on many tasks—fine motor skills, speech, and cognitive games. We could see a tinge of sadness and jealousy in Gwen's eyes. It was especially hard for Jennifer to witness such dynamics.

In the mornings Jennifer would call to see how my day was going. By the afternoon, she was inquiring when I'd be home. And by the time I crossed the doorstep at six or seven, she was passing off both babies to decompress herself. When we returned from Detroit, Jennifer transitioned from our family scrapbooker to a Creative Memories consultant to both quench her creative needs and to carve out time with other adults after days dominated by kids. Often, she would host a gathering at night or weekends. I relished these chances to take the kids on field trips to the mall, zoo, and museums, but found myself stretched without my own time to wind down. When I did have a quiet spell, it was the antithesis of my determined work persona. I seemed lazy, socially disengaged, and exhausted.

Eventually, Shell's growing distillates business supported expanding the group and, thankfully, narrowing my responsibilities to the Gulf and East Coasts. I thought I was doing well and continued to receive praise and recognition from my wise manager, Doug Arosell. Doug had a great way about him. He had tremendous commercial experience, but more importantly warm, rapport with staff in conveying tips and truths. Early in my role I once remarked that I hadn't sold a parcel of diesel as was planned because I didn't think the market was offering good value and that better options should develop the next day. He congratulated me for officially becoming a trader—for understanding my options and passing on the easy deal for the expectation of a better one.

However, as I shared with a co-worker at the time, I didn't quite feel comfortable with the entire role. "I like some of what I'm doing, but I just feel out of place. Picking up the phone and meeting others for lunches just isn't me." I could tell he couldn't quite relate, only suggesting I give it time. My transition from analytics and scheduling to more commercial and social skills was a struggle. At this point I could attribute my discomfort to my reserved nature, but I had not figured out how to properly cope with this stress. Perhaps this was just part of transitioning into a new role, but the constant nervousness held in the pit of my stomach made me feel that I was trying to "act" the part rather than "be" the part. It was confusing and tense.

My personal drive stretched me further out of my comfort zone. Over the next few years I learned a lot about the distillate markets and trading skills while our team accomplished many growth goals in order to challenge industry leaders. I got the sense my "fake it 'til you make it" approach was succeeding, as managers and co-workers alike praised my performance. Little did they know I would go home most nights and weekends, desperate to unwind my twisted nerves.

After a few years in distillates, in 1999 I shifted my talents to Shell's fuel oil trading team. My burgeoning attraction to business growth and to product blending was a great match. Blending involved not just buying finished product to supply fuel to utility plants, cruise ships, and cargo tankers on the oceans, but also to seek components to, in essence, *build* a finished fuel oil product in a more economical way. The blending aspect of fuel oil created new opportunities, often requiring more detailed analysis while offering the lure of greater profitability. Early on I could see this job and team would be unique.

Most past transitions were slow and challenging for me since it took time to warm up to new teams and tasks. Though I was always a proponent of a strong team, my reserved nature and junior status in Detroit and in distillates trading made it difficult to exert myself. However, my transition into fuel oil was quite smooth, aided by my growing confidence as a senior trader and our close-knit young team driven by common goals. After our first team manager opted to leave Shell shortly after my arrival, a goodbye lunch eventually left five of us at the bar until 4 PM, rotating glasses through the washer to the tune of over 130 shots of sweet, smooth Buttery Nipples. Beyond consciousness, I was poured into a taxi by my friend Robert and later dropped off at home. Somehow, I got to the back deck. I don't know how. Later that afternoon, Jennifer nudged my prostrate body and Madolyn pulled on her mom's shirt, saying "Look, Dad had chicken for lunch!" Sometime while I was passed out on the deck, I had thrown up my lunch and most of the drinks I had consumed had oozed through the deck slats.

This was a rare occurrence so Jennifer just snickered, thankful the kids were not really old enough to decipher the situation. It had been nine years since Jennifer and I met, and that security and companionship had enabled me to relegate alcohol to just a casual drink or two during social situations. This was really the first time in my 11-year career that my drinking intersected with work. It felt familiar and eased the pressure of delivery and social anxiety that was escalating in the role.

Our fuel oil team was filled with many ambitious, delivery-minded players. Everyone brought unique talents. Valerie had several years of trading experience at Shell and elsewhere. Aaron and I had many years of supply and trading experience as well. Dean came from another company with a long tenure of blending component trading. Adele brought her marketing talents to the team. Finally Jack, who started as a 14-wheeler truck driver before entering the energy industry as an inspector, joined our team as operator and later blender and trader. My drive, vision, and belief in the team helped bring us all together. My leadership status as senior trader also provided me with the authority I previously could not garner on my own. I leveraged this capacity to support my team-building mantra. Nightcaps downtown became the norm. I usually took the bus home but occasionally drove if we had a late dinner. Once we followed up our cocktails downtown with a few hours at another bar out west. During the drive, Jack bumped the back of my car, nudging me at a stoplight. All in fun, as long as no one got hurt. But my DUIs from 1984 and 1989 rang in my mind, yet I convinced myself I was fine and would always be careful.

The team struggled to deliver financial targets the first year, as we made some costly mistakes. I was so determined to help our close-knit team succeed that I even conspired with an industry competitor to influence pricing for a day by agreeing to artificially set a transaction above market levels. This violation of my own principles, let alone federal laws, weighed so heavily I had several rough nights with little sleep. I was embarrassed and scared, yet I could tell no one—neither my teammates nor Jennifer—and certainly didn't dare to repeat the act.

Despite our steep learning curve, we grew the business and developed many key skills. We gelled so well together, bonding as friends, tactfully challenging each other, and contributing to our ambitious strategy. The experience was very gratifying. By mid-year, we had not only exceeded our current annual target, but also recouped the shortfall from the previous year. Strangely, we celebrated with all the ladies in the group shaving the guys' heads bald on the trading floor. Yes, not quite the reward one might have envisioned, but another bonding moment for a team with such promise.

Not all was such well-planned fun. After hosting business guests at the Shell Houston Open PGA event, I found I was running late for a meeting and dinner with a terminaling company on the east side, about 20 miles away. I had shifted from beer to soda by mid-day, so I felt unencumbered for the drive. I darted to my car and hit the rush hour packed highway. However, I soon realized that in my haste I'd forgotten to go to the bathroom first. Concerned about being late, but reaching the "full" gauge, I creatively opted to relieve myself into a handy Mountain Dew bottle while driving. Sounds simple, but let me tell you, driving Houston highways while holding a bottle in one hand and myself in another while managing the gas pedal, all while standing up to aim down into a one-inch diameter hole, well, this should be an Olympic sport. It was my way of doing what needed to be done to meet an overly demanding and exhaustive schedule. While it was indeed memorable, it was yet another dangerous driving experience.

The fuel oil team atmosphere provided constant friends, filling a void since I had drifted away from Chris and Jim in 1991. Though my DUI experiences were not lost on me, my judgment was overwhelmed by the temptations of camaraderie, de-stressing, and team bonding. The primary instigators, Jack and I, headed to New Orleans for an industry event in 2003. Generally, when the two of us got together outside of the office we fed off each other's appetite for fun at all cost. So, this boondoggle started with drinks at the Houston airport at 7 AM, continued at the nearest French Quarter bar upon our arrival at 10 AM, and finished with Jack purging himself of red hurricanes all over my khakis at Pat O's piano bar around 3 AM the next day. I'm sure we went to some industry dinner, but I really can't remember amidst our drinking marathon.

Jennifer was certainly aware of the fun culture of our team. She enjoyed our semi-annual celebratory dinners with spouses, but she didn't know the extent and escalation of my drinking during this period, so no warning signs popped up and we both savored our different experiences.

On the heels of our team's strong financial performance and with a culture that was the envy of the trading floor, I became the team supervisor in late 2003. We continued to grow the business, expanding into other products and coastal regions in the US and Latin America. As the manager, I felt compelled to represent Shell at various industry conventions and cocktail hours. But these were never fun for me, despite often consuming copious amounts of alcohol to try to ease the discomfort. If I drank to overcome these events, I often ate to celebrate the completion of these hurdles. I always rose to the challenge to attend, but constantly fell short of my objective to strengthen key counterpart relationships. Yet our business was thriving. Perhaps the social shortcomings were more a perception within me rather than reality? Regardless, dampened by my overabundances, the fun and success of the role compensated for the stresses I endured.

It was a team of great chemistry, personality, and purpose. We struggled together, succeeded together, and celebrated quite well together. Always a believer in team and perhaps prepared to abuse my role to create such camaraderie, we celebrated with a lot of team dinners and annual holiday parties with spouses. Sometimes the parties got a bit out of control, with Jack spewing his dinner while dashing across Sullivan Steakhouse dining area toward the restroom, or Dean fertilizing the plant containers with his overflowing fruity drink. The *pièce de résistance* was our overnight party at Sara's Bed & Breakfast in the Heights in December of 2004. Spouses joined to celebrate yet another successful year. Jennifer was a perfect hostess, schmoozing with everyone and no doubt relishing her role as "First Lady of Fuel Oil." The theme was hip hop and every team member donned a necklace with a given hip hop name like "Masta Pixie Dust" (Dean, our blender), "Snoop Doggy A" (Adele, our marketer), and "Notorious J.A.C.K." (Jack). I was introduced by Adele in this way:

Steve's name was chosen to encompass all the many things he is to the team, all the many things that he does for the team, and our feeling of awe when we are in his presence because he is a machine and has endless energy and brainpower, and equally important he is a good friend to us all. So, Steve will be crowned "Brother ALL DAT."

We laughed, danced, drank, and bonded further. I told the team that night to "soak it all in. These are the best of times. They will not last long and may never return in our lives." My words were ominously prophetic.

The downfall of the team happened quickly and without warning—a clash of our relaxed, celebratory ambience and tightening industry regulations. After the Middle East oil embargo of 1973-74, oil prices jumped from $3 per barrel to $12. Decreased supply on the heels of the Iranian Revolution of 1979 catapulted oil prices above $20 for the first time and remained above $30 per barrel until the mid-80s, over 10 times the price levels less than a decade earlier. This volatility brought growth, profitability, and a cultural change to the energy markets. It was the norm for staff to leave the office for lunch and never come back. The industry would all mix at a favorite restaurant or bar and conduct business by phone or on napkins across the table while drinks flowed freely. However, declining prices by the late '80s tempered the daytime social scene just as I arrived at Shell in '88. An oil price dip below $15 in the late '90s, as well as an era of corporate consciousness on the heels of scandals and illegal deal structuring by Enron and other energy trading giants in the early 2000s, empowered big energy companies to adopt and enforce much stricter ethics guidelines. Shell joined that wave.

In late 2004 our human resources department identified Dean as violating Shell's new ethics policy. While the infractions (taking gifted baseball tickets from vendors for personal use and sending risqué jokes via e-mail from corporate accounts) were less than heinous, Shell was determined to enforce policy and set an example. Though the violations were largely pinpointed to one team member, the slack culture of the team was well known. I often attributed our demise to Kenneth Braman, a recent addition to our team, who distanced himself from the group, apparently in support of the investigation. He became our scapegoat. But in fairness, the problem revealed a lax culture that favored fun over form.

Ultimately, basic ethics policies were not followed. Though I was not involved or even aware of the specific violations at the time, as the team leader I had to take responsibility for the slack culture and ethics abuses. I had let my need for friendship and alcoholic therapy override my management mandate. By early 2005, Shell decided to disband the fuel oil team. My drinking buddy Jack was sent to Shell's Singapore office for a new three-year trading assignment and Dean, one of the catalysts for our team's success, was fired. Newcomer Kenneth was sent to the Netherlands for a trading role and, I suspect, partially to protect him from the snubbing he was receiving in Houston as a perceived mole.

My head was spinning. I was jerked back and forth between concern for my team—my friends—and my own fate. I was fortunate that my track record remained strong, and I had mentors who supported giving me another chance. My manager informed me, "We are finding you a good role. I will take care of you." Yet I was grieving over the dismantling of such a great team and the personal impact on so many. I also lamented the end of an exceptional period for me— tremendous business growth and financial success paired with friendships built in the trenches, none of which I had really enjoyed in my previous years at Shell.

CHAPTER 13: ROAD KILL

After a tumultuous end to my six years on the fuel oil team, I was offered a promotion to Global Trading Lead for Shell's liquefied petroleum gas (LPG: propane and butane) business based in London. This was another pre-ordained step up the trading hierarchy that I accepted with anticipation and trepidation. However, I left when my fuel oil team needed me most. Shell rewarded me with a promotion and an expat assignment while many others battled confusion and disarray. Yet my anguish was overridden by my need for self-preservation. I accepted the role and we prepared to relocate in the spring of 2005.

My dad instilled in me the ultimate responsibility as provider for the family. He had cut short his musical dreams and aspirations to return to Birmingham after school and Air Force service to work in his father's clothing shop and furnish for his family. Later, he worked long hours and weekends at his own store to support his wife and four kids. We led a middle-class existence, void of luxury but not lacking much of anything. He weathered crazy, drug-inspired adolescent children and his wife's battle with agoraphobia all to ensure their four kids had Bar/Bat Mitzvahs, went to college, and had beautiful weddings. He did it all at the expense of any retirement fund, a sensible work/life balance, and his own personal dreams.

He was a consummate provider who never complained about the burden or the consequences. While I could never suggest I am so noble or giving as he, I did seek to always deliver for my wife and kids. My need to offer safety, security and happiness to my family was so engrained in me that any risk to them weighed heavily. As a result, accepting this promotion to dig myself out of my own hole and then better provide for my family was not only the prudent choice, but also seemingly the only choice for me. Living up to this principle was so critical, but at what price?

As my chapter with the US fuel oil team faded away, the family and I were now catapulted into a life-changing experience. We were all excited to board the 10-hour transatlantic journey with our 21 bags that June day in 2005. From the start, it was such a bonding period for us. We literally knew no one but weren't afraid to explore. I considered our assignment "expat lite," given the locals spoke some dialect of English—albeit often barely discernable. Nevertheless, it was difficult to adjust to some aspects: eating different foods, dealing with stores closed on Sundays and at night, driving on the "wrong" side of the road, and sacrificing my 30-minute commute for a 90-minute commute each way. Adjusting to the seemingly year-round rainy, chilly, and overcast weather— not to mention giving up crispy bacon for a limp substitute— was certainly a mental challenge.

Though detaching from friends and routine was never easy, it was really a perfect time for our family to move. Jennifer was ready to take a break after nearly 10 years as a scrapbooking consultant and looked forward to pursuing a photography hobby with amazing European scenery as her backdrop. Gwen, now 10, had greatly benefited from physical and speech therapy in Houston. We always felt that Down syndrome was part of who she was, but it did not define or restrict her. She was an active, creative, loving, stubborn, and a quite capable young girl—when she wanted to be. She had certainly benefitted from her younger role model, Madolyn, who was nine when we moved. Madolyn had initially resisted our announcement to leave friends behind and move to England but was so resilient and flexible that she quickly came to embrace the experience and the travels ahead. Noah had joined both girls in 2002. At only three when we moved, Noah was cuddly, curious, and full of energy. The three kids kept us very busy and equally entertained. We knew a lot of change was in store for us. This was a unique family bonding experience sure to provide indelible memories.

As I began my first days of work, Jennifer and the kids were checking out the history, culture, and fun of London from our temporary corporate apartment on Kensington High Street. They planned day trips to the Science Museum, London Zoo, and Holland Park, visited London Tower and Greenwich Mean Time Royal Observatory, ate fish and chips and tuna and cucumber sandwiches, and rode the tube everywhere. I was so proud of their courage to explore this vast new city.

However, in July 2005 Jennifer and the kids were about to leave our apartment to tour the city when bombs exploded on the tube at the very station they were to pass through only an hour later. I saw the news from work and frantically called home to ensure everyone was safe and grounded for the day. With 52 killed and 700 injured, it was a cold reminder of the cultural melting pot and latent friction that permeated England. Numbed by years of conflict with Northern Ireland and the diversity of their city, the people of London were resilient and insistent that life goes on. Despite some personal hesitations that I think we were all too afraid to speak aloud, we followed the locals' lead and Jennifer and the kids were out on their next adventure the following day. A week after the attacks, all Britain stood still for a two-minute moment of silence. It was chilling to see people frozen in their paths, cars pulled roadside, trains stopped on the tracks. One hundred and twenty seconds later, everyone picked up their bags, put their hats back on, and chin-up resumed their day.

As late summer approached, our rental house in the countryside was ready. We shifted to lovely Virginia Water, a posh village with large overhanging trees and perfectly manicured hedges. Our home was the epitome of British life: dark brick with vines crawling up the front, complete with a Harry Potter-style front door with a rounded top and a long thick barrel key with one notch on the end. In August the kids entered school (Madolyn and Noah at the TASIS American School and Gwen at the British special needs school in nearby Portesbury).

One afternoon that month, Madolyn was the target of an ornery wasp that had snuck in through the back windows left ajar to generate a cool late summer breeze. Madolyn immediately called me in to assist. Despite flashbacks to Mom's shrieks from the upstairs bathroom years earlier, I grabbed a fly swatter and slithered into the room to survey the enemy. Jennifer pulled Gwen and Noah out of the room and closed the door, trapping us inside. With Madolyn as my cheerleader, I chased that sucker all over the room, standing on chairs and couches, gravitating from attack mode to defensive posture as this pissed-off flying ace took aim at me. The battle seemed to go on forever, with shrieks, screams, challenges, and taunts being tossed around. Madolyn ultimately laughed so much she lost control of her bladder and left a big puddle on the white carpet, but I was eventually victorious, swatting my worthy opponent in mid-air, proving that I was indeed smarter and stronger than something less than the size of my pinky finger. Victory!

However, we were not to stay inside very long. We were determined to tour the sights during our expected two- or three-year stay. We began planning our many family travels, taking advantage of the beneficial combination of frequent British-style week-long school breaks and the abbreviated American-style school year, both of which TASIS offered in order to entice ex-pat families to enjoy extensive travel. We saw amazing sites around our little village of Virginia Water, including magnificent Windsor Castle and the site of the 1215 signing of the Magna Carta on the nearby plush, sloping countryside.

As part of our indoctrination, Jennifer began reading some historical novels on Henry VIII and his unlucky wife, Anne Boleyn. The drama in the novels was elevated when we were able to visit the historic places these people once roamed. When Hever Castle finally reopened its doors after its winter hibernation, we decided to pay a visit to Henry and Anne's place. It was a typical dreary, drizzling day, which appeared fitting for Hever Castle.

After parking the car we navigated a maze of royal rose bushes looking for the entrance to the castle. Wearied by the expansive garden, we discovered a shortcut through the trees and down the hill. Jennifer led the way but quickly realized the weather conditions had turned the grassy slope into a muddy Slip 'N Slide. She took a spill and landed on her bottom, much to the excitement and laughter of the kids. So, it was my duty to save the lovely lady. However, despite careful footing, I bore the same fate as Jennifer, sliding down next to my fair maiden. When we both managed to get up, we realized we had a good coating of mud to contend with for the day.

Determined not to miss our much-anticipated tour, we dried off as best we could, covered up with our coats tied around our muddy waists, and proceeded to the castle for scones, tea, and finger sandwiches. The castle did not disappoint, with its cold stone hallways and its turrets holding many secrets. The highlight was Jennifer correcting a few stodgy British ladies on some of the history of Hever Castle and those who had walked the halls in much more challenging times. Their confusion, amazement, and finally embarrassment was quite a sight. As we left and the dried mud crumbled off, we agreed the day had been, well, quite British indeed.

While Jennifer was becoming an amazing photographer during our travels, capturing every moment for posterity, I was always anxious to get out front and experience the culture of our tours. I climbed 226 steps on Waterloo Monument in Belgium, hiked Mount Fuji, toured Hiroshima, scaled the Euromast of Holland, and sloshed through the waters of King David's underground waterway in Israel. So naturally, when we arrived at the Archaeolink Museum of medieval artifacts in Aberdeen, Scotland, I just had to try on a real coat of armor. I soon pictured myself on my trusty steed jousting with foes. When my reminiscing of past lives was over, I was ready to remove the armor and shuffle on to the next exhibit. However, the armor did not want to let go. I twisted and contorted my arms and back in efforts to remove myself. Akin to a Chinese finger trap that only tightens as one pulls and pleads for release, the more I struggled with the armor the more I became convinced I would never be free. Finally, I summoned my family who had already moved on to the next exhibit. After snapping the requisite photos, one would think my loving family would come to my rescue. But instead, they stood there laughing and pointing, amazed at how a 500-year-old piece of tin could bring their brave and courageous father to his knees. I was eventually released, but only after a few more photos.

Besides touring each corner of the United Kingdom, we also visited much of Europe and Israel, from the medieval castles of Prague and Croatia to the sloping Beersheba Desert of Israel. With the kids (10, 9, and 3 when we arrived in London), we were all mobile and impressionable. Madolyn became comfortable not only in international travel, subways, and passport lines, but more importantly she gained appreciation of the many differences—people looked and sounded different, and their cultures reflected unique traditions that contrasted from our middle-class Texan neighborhood—and that was indeed a good thing. What wonderful exposure to diversity and a chance to explore international history to its fullest.

Raised in the modern concrete fortress of Houston, where mid-twentieth century is considered historical and tourists seemingly are just transiting through for the attractions of New Orleans or San Antonio, communing with nature and amazing historical landmarks across Europe was a bit surreal. In front of the Roman Coliseum, Madolyn exclaimed flippantly: "It sure does look old and run down!"

Noah, being the youngest, had his own journey. He was truly "at one" (and two) with nature, dropping his drawers across the UK and Europe to pee in castles and wells, on the streets of Brussels near his namesake, the Mannequin de Pis, and in the ancient ruins of Israel. He even contributed fertilizer to the Scottish countryside, seated on the iron fence guarding the Picardy Stone. He definitely left his mark across Europe.

Sharing our family musical talents was another habit we adopted. I have the fondest of memories growing up with my folks singing their favorite show tunes and filling the house with music. Gwen was our self-designated rock star. Jennifer also shared a lovely, sweet voice. I myself claimed nothing, save the role of an amateur whistler. Meanwhile, Madolyn and Noah added great melody. Clearly, the kids' vocal gifts skipped my generation. Nevertheless, individual singing talents were far from a harmonizing family vocal unit. This was never more evident than during our vacation to the Spanish island of Gran Canaria. While we were driving from the sunny coast which hosted our camel rides to the snowy peaks just an hour away, the kids were lined up three across in the back seat. Suddenly, they broke into a uniquely off-tune rendition of "Mamma Mia"—all the rage in London in 2007. Each person in the car provided their own version, which, when blended with the others, must have summoned dogs from across the island.

Some of our most memorable trips included our first drive to the Continent to visit the majestic castles and stone streets of Bruges, Belgium and our initial visit to the Eiffel Tower and class of Paris. Our first Thanksgiving overseas, however, featured a takeout KFC feast in our hotel room the night before touring Dover Castle, overlooking the famed white cliffs. We then caught a ferry ride across the English Channel for the drive south, followed by a full day of touring the beaches of Normandy, France. I was excited to see the jagged shoreline where thousands scaled the precipices to eventually free Europe from the death and tyranny of Nazi Germany, but everyone else was riddled with full-body colds that emitted fluids from eyes, nose, and mouth. I couldn't tell whether they were suffering from a near death bodily experience or if they were merely bored to death. Either way, we cut our tour short and I learned a lasting lesson that weekend: I must balance history with play or else misery will be our unwanted guest.

One weekend we left Gwen and Noah with our trusted part-time nanny, Donna, and Jennifer and Madolyn joined me after my business meetings in Poland. We trembled at the chilling Auschwitz concentration camp and the moving visuals of the old Warsaw ghettos. We were engrossed in Poland's amazing museums, which paid homage to the survivors of both. It was a solemn weekend to share together.

Not surprisingly, our favorite trip was our Mediterranean cruise in the summer of 2006. Our ship sailed from Barcelona alongside the French Riviera, down the western coast of Italy with stops in Florence, Pisa, Rome, and the Amalfi Coast, before visiting Santorini Island, Athens, and Croatia and finally concluding in Venice. The trip was so surreal. Each city oozed with history, fantastic rich foods, and the warmth of our local hosts—all while enjoying the comforts and convenience of our Celebrity cruise ship. After 12 days on board, we were tempted to stay on for a return trip. That's always a good sign, yet we had to fly back to London to plan our next adventure.

Our most impactful trip was our 10-day excursion through Israel in 2007. Jennifer had been to Israel as a teen, but for the rest of us it was our first time. We toured the massive plateau of Masada, which was the last Judean fortress to fall to the Roman onslaught in 73 AD, as well as the buoyant saltwater of the Dead Sea below.

The desert craters of Makhtesh Ramon south of Beersheba in the Negev Desert provided an unexpected oasis to the senses: the silky soap derived from the desert plants, the stomach-wrenching thrill of an off-road Jeep ride, and the relaxing smooth taste of Bedouin tea shared with our host, Ziv, at his ranch.

The well-preserved historical ruins of Beit She'an and Tel Megiddo brought us back to the pre-Bronze Age, over 5,000 years ago, to envision how Canaanites and their periodic conquerors lived on the column-lined stone streets and excavated buildings that still remained.

Toward the end of our trip, we finally arrived in Jerusalem to walk the sites of the Old City with its Jewish, Muslim, Armenian, and Christian Quarters side by side. We were overwhelmed by our emotional visit to the historical jewel of the Western Wall, the last remaining wall of the Great Temple that rose to the Al-Aqsa Mosque on the Temple Mount. The pinnacle of our trip was joining a synagogue for Shabbat services on Friday night. As we walked the main road to services, people streamed out of the side streets, often holding hands as they strolled toward the synagogue. Once inside the service was uniquely spirited, with loud, boisterous singing and dancing. Locals and tourists alike shared their energy, belief, and devotion to God and to country.

During our trip, I journaled often, ultimately noting three observations. First was the innate comfort and belongingness. As a Jew who grew up in the Deep South, I never appreciated such a sense of community. Frankly, I never realized I lacked such sentiment. But in Israel, we didn't need to hide our Jewish identity, our Magen David stars on our necklaces, our traditions or our heritage. Though the people of Israel were used to being surrounded by enemies who planned for their demise, inside the country's borders they felt safe to practice their beliefs in peaceful passion.

Second, because of such comfort—and despite rocket fire and the constant potential for bus bombs and terrorists—we all had an uncanny sense of safety and security. It flew in the face of logic, perhaps because the locals did not let such fear ruin their day or govern their life. I sensed that if it did, they would have lost the independence they so cherished.

Finally, I found the amalgamation of different cultures—Jewish, certainly, spanning all reaches of the world from Yemen to Ethiopia to Russia and the US, but also Muslims, Christians, Baha'i and others living side by side. I'm sure there were social and political disputes amongst citizens just as in any country, but contrary to the belief and perhaps intense desire of many outside the borders of Israel, these groups generally seemed to live in some sort of harmony and peace with each other. What great lessons to be learned about the world and about my own pursuit for harmony and peace within myself.

Meanwhile, back in London I had to pinch myself daily when I walked to work from Waterloo Station, crossing the

Golden Jubilee Bridge with St. Paul's Cathedral to my right and British Parliament to my left.

Yet this life of adventure and family bonding was in stark contrast to my work experiences.

CHAPTER 14: STRETCHED

With our extensive family travels as a backdrop, I was adjusting to Shell Trading's London headquarters and my new job. The office was different—more structured and a bit aloof, perhaps a reflection of the blended British and Dutch cultures that pervaded the workplace. The London office dress code forced me to shelve my Houston casual attire in lieu of the more formal coat and tie of Shell's trading hub. I opted to collect and wear fun ties: ties depicting historical landmarks from our many travels (including Rome's Trevi Fountain and the walls of Dubrovnik, Croatia—home of the first neckties), as well as ties heralding baseball, Mickey Mouse, and the American flag–my subtle way to express myself. My collection received many stares, but rarely created a friendly introduction or connection with my new co-workers. Still, my global role offered opportunity, both to make a difference professionally and to challenge myself personally.

After all, this role was the pinnacle of product trading. One of only six global product leader roles and just twice removed from the President of Trading. I was excited but frankly somewhat shocked that a reserved, nervous guy like me had made it this far. But management certainly had shown a lot of faith in me, especially over the last few months. Perhaps I really was deserving of their praise and this role. Maybe this would be the job where I would beam with confidence and overcome my shyness.

Upon arrival at the 80 Strand office, I met my London trading team and many of my contemporary Global Leaders for other products such as gasoline, distillates, and fuel oil. I was replacing Oscar, who had been in the global LPG role for six years and had developed strong relations across the team, but had also let the business model become a bit stale over his term. My new manager, Erwin Walters, Vice President of Products Trading, was an American who had arrived from Houston a few years earlier. My mission, as presented by Erwin, was to take this comparatively small business ($25 million per year, relative to $200 million per year for most other products) and grow the scope and the bottom line. Our business spanned the globe with staff in Houston, London, Rotterdam, Dubai, Singapore, Manila, Tokyo, and Barbados. As Global Leader, I was to coordinate this team of about 25 traders to develop strategies that the staff would then leverage through short- and long-term contracts to buy, sell, and transport LPG around the world. I had salivated over growth opportunities in my previous trading roles, so I immediately dove in to identify issues and strengths of our team while building my knowledge of the LPG industry.

Though I found the challenges of the new role invigorating, it also proved stressful. The new location, product, and team provided a sense of personal chaos that was heightened by my immediate need to build rapport with people of so many diverse and distant cultures. Phone conversations were insufficient. Suddenly my international travel became 50% of my time. My most common trips were west to Houston and Barbados and east to Tokyo, Manila, and Singapore. In addition to my customarily slow process of developing relations within my team, I was also challenged with introductions to even more diverse and experienced industry leaders, who were cautiously watching our competitive moves.

The transition from logistical and analytical tasks to commercial roles in the mid-'90s was now moving toward more strategic and stakeholder management tasks in 2005. It was a natural progression during a career in trading and supply, but as I reflected during one of my many overnight flights to Singapore, I was indeed far from my comfort zone. My days were filled with staffing, internal relationship building, and strategic planning. Our business was extraordinarily people focused. So I was decidedly involved in all the hiring, training, and aligning of a cohesive, high functioning team. Though the culture of my previous team was obviously flawed, replicating the trust, camaraderie, and financial success was my goal.

As had become typical, when faced with such challenges, I pursued them with vigor and obsession. By the end of 2005 we had re-staffed key positions, shifted our business focus to the expanding eastern market with new leadership in Singapore, and began to build trading skills within the team. With these tough restructuring decisions implemented, we started to deliver on our financial objectives. My compulsive drive created new projects, including striving to bring more value to the local Nigerian LPG markets. Perhaps I was stretching myself thin, but this unique prospect was entrepreneurial and exciting.

Meanwhile, developing relations with the other Global Product Leaders (who could be both a source of knowledge and experience, but also a source of competition for Shell resources) soon became my biggest frustration. I was handicapped in the battle over staffing and financial capital, which all product businesses found critical for success. The other teams were larger, well established, and had built well-deserved clout given their contributions to Shell Trading's targets. I beseeched them to make some trading talent available for transfer to my young team to help ignite further growth. However, since their bonuses were based on their own team's performance, they all appeared quite resistant. As Erwin was promoted from Products VP to Trading President, our new products leader, Harold Rudman, was quickly indoctrinated into the ways of the world by the larger product books, and thus he was not prepared to compromise them by stripping talent to support our fledgling business. I often dwelled on this obstacle. My social anxiety and aversion to conflict kept me from improving my arguments or my approach. I was neither successful nor prepared to mentally move on and make the best of our resources. Thus, I assumed the character of the downtrodden victim—never an impressive persona to new staff or colleagues.

In the meantime, as our internal strategy took shape, I began visiting more customers and attending many industry events sprinkled around the world, from Taiwan to Peru, Nigeria to Italy. Sometimes my trips were brief and very business focused, other times I had the opportunity to experience the food, nightlife, and history of worlds I had barely heard of before. These additional travels provided a great chance to see remarkable sites including Mount Fuji outside Tokyo and Machu Picchu in the remote Sacred Valley of Peru.

The latter was especially inspiring as my team member, Oliver, and I toured the scenery with our guide, learning of the struggles of over 20,000 Incas to assemble the temples, homes, and agricultural terraces that clung to the plush green mountainside. Amazingly, Machu Picchu was not completed before being mysteriously abandoned around 1500, sparing it from the conquering Spaniards of 1536. American Hiram Bingham rediscovered it during his expeditions of 1911-15 in search of ancient Inca temples. I reflected on having a similar task to Bingham: taking a dormant jewel (LPG Trading) and reinvigorating it until it would one day be recognized for its impact and beauty. But neither of our tasks were simple or without frustrations.

After an amazing weekend in the countryside of Peru, Oliver and I arrived in Lima for an industry LPG conference. I was thrust into the heart of my kryptonite: cocktail socials with people I hardly knew, amidst a sea of seasoned LPG veterans. Furthermore, I was also tasked with introducing Oliver to key counterparts. I was overwhelmed with the responsibility and fearful failure would expose my weakness as his team leader.

"Hello," I interjected as I nudged us into a small group conversation. We often received no more than stares, as they appeared offended at our intrusion into their friendships.

Feeling any confidence slipping, I took advantage of a brief moment of silence. "Hello, this is Oliver and I'm Steve. We're with Shell's LPG team." A bit awkward, but perhaps we were now part of the conversation? However, often they would just nod and continue within their own group.

Other times they might lob a question our way: "How do you see natural gas production impacting LPG supply in Latin America?"

Oh, boy. I was never one to shy away from a direct question. It felt like an opportunity to earn our way into the group and seemed better than idle chitchat. However, as a newcomer to the market, my rambling response made it clear I had failed their test. Perhaps I was just paranoid, but I sensed others picked up on this and returned to their discussion of old times together and their plans for dinner or drinks later that evening. Clearly, I had not earned an invitation to either. Oliver seemed to sympathize with my struggles as I abruptly backed out of the group, only to have to walk the floor in search of a welcoming face to approach next, which rarely presented itself. I grabbed another drink to try to relieve the tension, but I could not drink enough that night to soften my approach. I recognized making these connections was a key part of my role as Shell's LPG Trading representative, so skipping these sessions was a tempting but not acceptable option. So I continued to torment myself for hours that seemed like days of pain.

I wrote an email to Jennifer after that evening: "It zapped my energy just trying to maintain such a façade. Jennifer, I describe myself lately as puny, timid, socially regressive, lazy, stressed, and basically fragile. I've never prided myself as a social butterfly, nor do I care to. But lately I feel like more of a social wallflower. Unable to hold even the basic social conversation let alone to strike up a discussion of any depth."

Realizing the depressed tone of my letter and not wanting to scare Jennifer from halfway around the world, I tried to reassure her: "However, I must emphasize, I'm okay. I'm not going off the deep end." But in reality I felt like I was. In the pit of my stomach, I was scared. I felt like I was losing my use of basic logic and communication skills. I was overcome by fear every day: of people, of losing, of speaking, of being quiet, of not providing, of not being enough, of not being courageous.

Though I had always been shy, this was different and more desperate. When I returned to London I reached out for help with a therapist. After hearing my stories and struggles, she branded me with social anxiety. She described it as "shyness on steroids." I could get worked up just anticipating a social gathering. After awkward interactions, I often felt others easily detected my clunky skills like a wagon hobbling along with a broken wheel. I sensed others were constantly judging me, perhaps even to the point of ridicule. I was often frozen up from this fear.

I reflected on my own timid nature during these introspective sessions. I thought of Mom's battle with mental health and agoraphobia, specifically. As a kid, I'd always viewed Mom as an extrovert. She was social with friends and always on the phone with relatives. However, perhaps she was more of an introvert, pushed out of her comfort zone by social norms. Even more so in the '70s, there seemed to be an expectation of being prim and proper, and regularly dining and dancing at the local clubs. Perhaps my social dancing at these cocktail hours was not much different. Maybe this stress is what pushed Mom unwillingly toward agoraphobia?

Agoraphobia is not only the fear of open spaces but also of social situations. I think it can be an extreme form of introversion, promoted by emotional fear, panic, and embarrassment. Much as I was discovering my shyness had elevated to anxiety, could my introversion elevate to agoraphobia? I'd seen the damage agoraphobia had on Mom and the whole family. Such torment scared me a lot. It was a lot to handle at once.

I'm generally a resilient person who tries to put on a mask of confidence and business capability. I didn't intend to adopt this "fake it 'til you make it" strategy but had become dependent on it to survive. Yet with so many obstacles, this assignment necessitated an extreme use of disguise. In my journal I asked myself: "Is it time to stop faking and go to a place of natural comfort?"

When faced with such stress I tended to bury myself in addictive behaviors. Thus my compulsive nature drove me to work longer hours, often 7 AM to 7 PM in the office plus late-night calls to other locations after my long commute home. I lived with my Blackberry at my bedside, the blinking red light drawing me to check email and voicemail as I tossed and turned throughout the night. I stepped up my international travel even further in an effort to move my agenda along. However, my travel was also driven by the hope to escape the politics of the London office and the guilty feeling that I was abandoning my duties at home.

Unbeknownst to me, given my own spiraling condition, Jennifer was dealing with her own issues. Though Shell's ex-pat package had cured our family budget problems, Jennifer was once again left to run all the errands and tend to the three kids and the house. She might have been used to my long work hours in the past, but this time life was more complicated. Shopping might lead her to a half dozen stores to buy what she could have bought at a grocery store or Target back home. Rather than us splitting duties, Jennifer was always called upon for the kids' school and extracurricular activities and had to console the kids who missed their dad as well.

Jennifer occasionally joined the ex-pat ladies' outings but was inclined to feel like an outsider to the socialites. We both suffered levels of shyness and introversion. Yet, I was pulled away due to work obligations, leaving us both to manage our similar afflictions by ourselves. Regrettably, I was not there to reciprocate the comfort and support Jennifer had so often shared with me throughout my career. Jennifer later noted: "I was living day-to-day as a single mom." How heartbreaking to put her through such anguish, but I was desperately focused on myself at the time.

In between my long work hours and global trips, we always packed up for intensive family travels. We never spent a break at the house. We toured Wales and Scotland, drove around Europe, and flew to Israel and other places. We never stayed in one place but scheduled numerous stops to cram in as many sites as possible. We led a life of extremes. I did know the damage I was causing. I just chose not to address it because, on the surface, our personal travel quenched my guilt at not spending time with the family. Yet it did not support a healthy balance but rather a cumulative level of tension, not just for me, but for Jennifer and the kids as well.

My work experience was eroding me from a successful team manager in Houston to an overwhelmed global manager. Unlike the medieval armor I struggled to escape from in Scotland, my armor as a dependable and present father and a resilient and determined Shell leader was rusting away from the edges.

Over the years I developed a strong aversion to conflict, largely from periods observing constant bickering between my mom and my headstrong sisters growing up at the Crestbrook house. Now every week seemed to be filled with conflict—with my manager, my peers, some of my staff, and an occasional competitor concerned about Shell flexing its muscles in their market.

Success was slow and painful.

My retreat became my long transcontinental travels. Every couple of weeks I found myself on flights lasting six to 20 hours. Comforted in first class with a good meal, free flowing wine, plentiful chocolate, no blinking Blackberry, and no badgering stakeholders, I took refuge. I rarely slept on these long flights, desperately wanted to take full advantage of such an escape. Occasionally I had the opportunity to stay in amazing spots during the weekend in the middle of my two-week business trips out east. These were always solo weekends, which satisfied my venturesome curiosity, but more importantly fulfilled my need for solitude to balance the workweek strain. In September of 2006, I had such a chance to see the overwhelming history and emotions of Hiroshima in between a visit to Tokyo and a week in Singapore.

Upon arriving from Tokyo via the Shinkansen bullet train, I spent a couple of hours touring the Hiroshima Peace Park Museum. To see the horrible death, disfigurement, and utter annihilation of an entire city and its people was chilling. After walking around the city, I sat by the calm banks of the Motoyasu River next to the Hiroshima Peace Park to journal on the horrific scenes captured in the museum and the perspective it brought to my personal struggles:

September 02, 2006

I feel overwhelmed and exhausted. I think I either have to overcome my fears and beat this social anxiety or prepare myself to move on to a job more suitable for my style and talents. After all these years, I don't think I will change who I am. But how can I walk away from this senior job, from the security it provides me? A change might be the right thing to do, but it's so much to consider. I feel like I'm at a crossroad, just standing here, unable to move.

I parked my sadness and joined a packed house to watch the Hiroshima Carp professional baseball team beat the Yakult Swallows 5-2, to the delight of excited fans waving their streamers and pompoms, all with the pain of World War II providing the backdrop just over the left field fences.

After wrapping up an intense weekend, I buttoned up my emotions and pressed on to our 2006 global LPG team meeting in Singapore. While strategy, coordination, and engagement plans with key customers were the agenda, I also planned a relaxing full team dinner that evolved into a long evening of drinking for the remaining five diehards. In the back of my mind, I knew this was not work appropriate, especially in light of my role in the compliance issues with my fuel oil team just a couple of years earlier. Yet this had always been the best way I knew to cut past the business formality and truly develop some lasting trust and rapport and, perhaps more importantly, it afforded me the opportunity to escape from work stresses and just relax, even for a bit. So that evening turned into a long night as we closed the hotel tavern around 2 AM and then climbed over the vacated bar to grab several bottles of wine and head to the beach.

On the beach, stories and laughter led to bonding. Around 3 AM we peered off into the hazy, moonlit bay at a distant island. A few of us drunkenly agreed to swim to the island, wine bottles in hand. Stripped to our underwear, Mike, Sam and I began the journey. It seemed like a struggle against the waves until we finally dragged up on the shore of our newfound island. Once we caught our breath, we realized we hadn't brought a corkscrew or glasses so, resourcefully, we busted the bottles against a rock and poured the wine into our mouths.

I must say Shell was a fabulous company in many ways, and truly a safety leader in the energy industry. But I think we violated nearly every safety rule that night. We were lucky we didn't cut ourselves, get drunk beyond recognition, drown off the beach, or get arrested in this foreign land. I tend to dismiss such concerns when drinking in order to buy some comfort and relaxation, but there could have been some real consequences for such unsanctioned behavior. I considered myself quite lucky to remain employed with Shell and, in some cases, to be alive.

Our evening ended on the island about 5 AM, after which we swam back to shore in time for the three of us to clean up and head to our team breakfast and day of meetings. Later, at a meeting break in the afternoon, with the sunlight glaring down on Singapore, the three of us went outside for a few minutes to stare out at our evening conquest. We all burst out in laughter. The island we struggled to reach was probably no more than 50 yards away, and I wouldn't be surprised if we could have walked there rather than swam. Yet the strains at work and in my head were no illusion.

CHAPTER 15:
BREAKING POINT

The stress for success was definitely taking its toll on my body. I was visiting my primary care physician every month with a new ailment: sciatica down my left leg, back pain, red rashes on my face and head, itching, shingles behind my ears, poor sleep—not to mention I was gaining weight rapidly. I arrived in London in '05 a husky 220 but by 2007, despite working out in the Shell gym a few times a week, I was topping the scales above 250. In the office, I was drinking six Diet Cokes each day. A co-worker noticed my habit and remarked in the café line, "I read an article on how that NutraSweet stuff will kill you. You should really spare your liver and stop those drinks." I shrugged off the comment. I was in no position to make healthy choices. Besides, NutraSweet concerns would certainly be low on my list anyway. I had fallen into a destructive pattern. I instinctively reached for alcohol to prime myself for the stress of social events and to endure such gatherings. Afterwards, I gorged carbs and desserts to celebrate surviving another meeting or luncheon.

Though I never drank alone, I was typically binging food by myself—on the train home, on late-night kitchen runs, and especially during business trips. I would joke to myself that I was a solid quarter of the way to being cut out of a house. But as I continued to shift from one belt hole to another before I could even wear them in, I knew this would have severe consequences. I just couldn't muster the courage to change my situation. Worse than my expanding pant size and rotund look was the plummeting confidence and self-esteem which, when mixed with my timid nature, made my bundle of stress even more overwhelming.

Not surprisingly, my doctor attributed all my visits to stress. "Our bodies are amazing, interlocking machines," he said. The tension I experienced was taking its toll. "I can try to treat the aches and pains, but the only way to alleviate them is to relieve the stress. I can't do that for you." I reflected on my thoughts in Hiroshima but still could not drive myself to force a change that could resolve my growing list of symptoms. So, I coped as best I knew how: drinking and eating while pushing myself even harder to meet the demands of my global role.

In the summer of 2007 yet another trip east was on the schedule. I spent a couple of days visiting my team of four in Manila during which my local supervisor announced he was resigning from Shell after 15 years to follow his dream: karaoke bar owner. My initial thought was, *this is crazy*. Who leaves a good paying job at a company like Shell to pursue a hobby? Later I realized how much I truly respected and envied Joey's clear vision and determination to escape from an obligation to pursue happiness. This was against all norms and expectations. How brave!

After Manila I flew to Cambodia for a personal weekend. This jaunt was the antithesis of the norm for me, someone who scheduled every trip to the hour and took few travel risks. I landed in Siem Reap's small, dusty airport with only a hotel reservation and a guidebook. But the allure of visiting 12th century ancient ruins that had just recently been revealed after explorers peeled back the overgrown jungles was too much to pass up. When I exited the airport, I was met with several taxi invitations. One seemed a bit more personal, so I told him the name of my hotel. Once we got in his 1970s Toyota, he introduced himself as Cantu. He asked my plans for my stay. Normally, I'm quite reluctant to reveal such details for fear of some sinister intent. However, here and now, desperate for some relief, I could not muster the strength to properly assess options or risks. Once I shared my desire to see temple ruins, Cantu offered to chauffeur me around for my two days. The cost was only $25 US and I could pay when he returned me to the airport. Cautiously, I accepted this great deal.

"If you have time, sir, it is almost sunset. I can take you to the Phnom Bakeng Temple and you can climb to the top for the best view around. It is definitely amazing!" I was all in at this point, so off we went. Once parked at the foot of the temple, I looked up at the hundreds of people and many hundreds of steps. I began the climb. The heat, compounded by my poor fitness, weighed me down and necessitated many stops to catch my breath.

Finally, I arrived at the top for a glorious view of the deep orange setting sun cutting over the bright green treetops from the jungle below. I sat down to absorb the splendor of the scene. So serene and peaceful. I scanned the diverse crowd of onlookers and journaled a bit in between gazes at the magnificent view.

Once the sun set, I watched some of the crowd—locals and travelers alike—begin to head down. As I eyed one visitor burdened with a heavy backpack, I realized Cantu—if that really was his name—was down below with all my luggage in the back of his car. He could take off and leave me stranded with nothing. Was that truly his big payoff? Was this a scam? My stomach twisted as I peered down, trying to find Cantu and his Toyota amongst the sea of matchbox cars. I could not.

I set aside my worries in order to find the best path down. Locals were offering elephant rides down a steep, winding path on the side of the temple. That sounded like a unique adventure with far less toll on my knees. However, the guide said I was too heavy for them to take me down. Too heavy for an elephant? Really? Frustrated, I began the trudge down, step by step. As I neared the bottom, I anxiously scanned for Cantu, but to no avail. Panic returned. Were my fears now realized? Lost without my clothes and my work bag in Cambodia? Fleeting thoughts flashed through my head.

Suddenly, Cantu appeared in front of me. He saw the panic in my face and said, "Do not worry, sir. I just had to park to the side." He pointed me back to the Toyota. Relieved, I thanked him for the suggested stop and we headed to the hotel. Over the next couple of days, he showed me many other unique Temples as well as Tonle Sap Lake, containing dozens of elevated huts which served as houses, schools, and stores which in the summer rainy season were only accessible by water taxi. This weekend was a silver lining in my long business travels.

Leaving this escape behind on Sunday, I caught a flight to Singapore for a few days of meetings before heading home. I was looking forward to catching up with my fuel oil friend, Jack, who was still stationed in Singapore. By Tuesday my tranquil weekend in Cambodia was swept aside by stressful meetings with my new Singapore team lead, Dieter. After years soliciting for strong talent from other products books, the Chemical Feedstocks global lead, Nigel, offered Dieter to come to LPG. Though experienced, Dieter was also quite headstrong and egotistical. His friendly bond with Nigel also concerned me, given my discomfort with Nigel's brash and somewhat pompous style. But after petitioning for talent I felt pressured to accept the offer. Yet from our first meeting I could tell we would be head-butting often on strategy and staff development approaches.

I was relieved to wind down with Jack over dinner and

drinks after work. As is customary with Jack, however, the evening was light on dinner and heavy on drinks. "Let's order some sushi to start, Jack,"

"I've already ordered a couple of bottles of warm sake. Let's think about sushi later. Want some wine too?"

Exasperated, but seeking some release from the day's stress, I relented and started to make waste of the first bottle of sake.

The grumbling of an empty stomach along with empty sake and wine bottles took its toll. Though I gestured back to the menu at times, I was equally guilty of the alcohol spree. Somehow, we drifted into a rare argument, the topic of which neither of us could later recall.

Well inebriated and frustrated by an evening that did little to soothe the tension from the day's meetings, it was time to go. We said our abbreviated and tempered goodbyes and I hailed a taxi. That's about the last I remember of the evening. I can recall—or have at least been told of—a handful of blackout situations in my life dating back to my first drink at 11 and passing out on the back deck in Houston years later, but this was the scariest. This was the first time I blacked out in a foreign country, let alone one with rigid social norms, rules, and severe penalties.

I woke up the next morning to my ringing phone alarm. As my eyes slowly opened, I found myself sprawled out face down on my hotel room floor. I looked around as faint recollection of our sake shots flashed in my mind. I rolled over to pat myself down, locating my wallet and keys in the process. I looked around the room for my work bag but didn't see it. I pulled myself up. My pace quickened as each glance around the room failed to find my bag with computer inside. I called Jack in desperation.

"Jack? Steve. Do you remember seeing my work bag? I can't find it anywhere. Maybe I left it in the taxi. Or at the restaurant?"

"Calm down, I have your bag. You left it at the restaurant."

"Oh, shit. Thanks, man. Do you remember what happened last night? I really can't remember anything after we split."

"Not really." Jack seemed to shrug it off, still dejected by the odd argument, which clearly still stuck in his head at the time. "I'll leave your bag at your desk. I gotta go."

I slowly began moving to get ready to go to the office, all the while trying to piece together any recollections of how my night ended. Suddenly, a picture popped in my head. Just one. I was seated in a rigid plastic chair and it appeared I was at a police station. People were scurrying around behind the counter. No one took much notice of me. I can recall nothing else. It could have been a figment of my imagination, but the clarity of that one moment leads me to believe I was indeed there. Why? For how long? How could I have been released, given Singapore's police society with little patience for foreigners breaking their rules? How did I then get to the hotel room? I don't know.

The evening was very disturbing. If I was so drunk in this place, I could have been hurt, jailed, killed. That night, I crossed the line. I spent the last couple of nights of my trip in my room, still rattled from Tuesday night's memories.

A couple of months later, in October of 2007, my regional lead Mike hosted the London-based team for dinner at OXO Tower on the South Bank in London. The food was delicious, and the wine flowed freely until about 11 PM. As was always the case in London, when the fun was over everyone headed off in different directions to catch various trains home. I marched off to catch my hour-long southwest train from Waterloo Station out to Surrey. Unfortunately, the excessive wine mixed with my unfamiliarity with the South Bank led me to wander the area for well over an hour. Too inebriated to be worried, I started texting Mike and later Jennifer of my whereabouts in search of Waterloo. With some guidance from Mike, I eventually found my way to the station. The next day, Mike and I chuckled as he read back my texts.

Jennifer, on the other hand, was worried and concerned. In my drunken condition, I had given Jennifer a peek inside my world. She was terrified. "People get mugged or worse on the South Bank every night. How much did you drink?"

"It wasn't that much. It was just late and I didn't know my way around the area." Despite my flippant response, she knew I'd drunk a lot that night. Though I never felt compelled to share my drunken nights in Singapore, her intuition and my rising weight suggested to her that it was getting dangerous for my health and safety. I downplayed the situation, hoping not to worry her, but these extreme evenings were starting to add up. I was scaring myself.

A few months back, Jennifer and I had scheduled a getaway to Prague for the following weekend. I was looking forward to some relaxation and exploration together in this mystical Czech city that had persevered despite regional and world wars that had swirled around it for centuries. It was an appropriate scene now, given our latent friction from my South Bank excursion just a few days earlier.

Finally, in our hotel after the flight, we had the most candid discussion of our relationship.

"You scared me this week. You could have been killed! You are drinking a lot. You are gone a lot. I get it, work is demanding and difficult, and I want to help."

I tried to shrug off the comments and downplay her concerns. "This job has been really difficult. It's not what I expected at all. The bickering with management… You just don't know the stresses of the job. I don't want to bring all this work crap home with me. I don't want to burden you, and frankly I just don't want to think about it when I'm not at work."

"You're right. I don't know all the details. But you aren't sharing. We hardly see you. And you aren't taking care of yourself—or us," she unloaded. "Steve, things need to change!"

Jennifer and I rarely seemed to have differences that rubbed either of us wrong. Since we met we were always on the same page, with the same dreams and view on life. We also tended to compromise rather than defend and debate positions. We rarely lashed out or fought but processed situations quietly, in our own ways. It's how we were both raised. So I recognized it was monumental for her to raise these issues. It took a lot of courage for Jennifer to step up and confront the situation, underscoring the amount of pain I was putting her through.

I paused. I knew she was exactly right. It was time for me to swallow my pride and let her in.

"I'm sorry. It's not been easy. This is not what I thought this job would be. I really don't like it. I miss you and the kids. I don't know what to do. We probably have another year or two on this assignment. After that I think it's time to go back to Houston and for me to leave the trading rat-race and find a different kind of role in Shell."

"Two years? That's a long time."

Jennifer listened. She tried to understand. But I could tell she didn't like the idea of another year or two of this life. Was this the "catch" she had feared when our relationship started off so seamlessly?

I sat down on the edge of the bed facing away from her and I wept. I was so ashamed. "I'm just not sure what to do. I eat and drink to dull the pain. I'm not sure how to deal with all the stress. I need your help to figure this out."

"I want to help, Steve. Together, we'll get through this."

We held each other, crying together. The courage Jennifer showed had brought us to another juncture. We cleaned up, closed the door to our hotel room, and walked into the Old Town along the Charles River as snow began to fall. Jennifer was once again saving me from myself. Now I needed the courage to make my own changes.

A couple of months later we all went back to the States for the holidays—a rare sacrifice of European travel time. Family could see the exhaustion etched on our faces. Our top 10 travel list was long complete and we were missing the conveniences of home. We were certainly ready for some return to normalcy. As another year began Jennifer and I didn't talk much about our Prague discussion, but I vowed to control my drinking and evaluate my travel schedule to try to find a more balanced life. Sure, we still shared the love we had nurtured for decades, but there was a new sense of urgency to solve the problem hanging over us.

CHAPTER 16: NUMB

Once we returned from the States in early January, I adjusted my work hours to get home by 6 PM. That left me with more phone calls at night, but Jennifer and I both felt added time at home would help everyone. Though I thinned out my travel schedule, by mid-January I was headed to Singapore for a week with the team. Given my last trip and my determination to adhere to my agreement with Jennifer to limit my drinking, I made no effort to let Jack know of my plans to be in Singapore. I've never been able to moderate drinking with Jack.

After my arrival, Dieter and I met with the team to discuss 2008 goals. I could sense an air of discomfort from the staff in the meeting. I grabbed coffee with some of the team members later.

"How are things?" I inquired.

Hampered by their Far Eastern timidity, the guys didn't want to air dirty laundry—especially about Dieter, their new manager whom I had hired myself in the fall. But I'd known these guys for a couple of years. I'd hired most of them during our buildup of the eastern business in 2005. I could see by their distant stares that things weren't going well.

"Listen, Dieter has a lot of trading knowledge," I offered. "His style is different but can drive us toward growth in the east. But I want to make sure you guys are all working as a cohesive, respectful team, yes?"

"We've got a ways to go," one mumbled.

"I understand. Give it some time. Let's keep in touch."

Later in the week Dieter and I interviewed candidates for a new trader position. Though we both sought an upgrade of talent, our evaluation of candidates underscored our different styles.

"What are you looking for in a new trader?" I asked.

"A strong, experienced trader that will shake things up with the rest of the team. I want a trader that will follow my lead with emphasis on paper trading."

"Yes, we certainly have a chance to increase talent. Be careful with the team dynamics. You've got solid traders in your team. They function best in the local, niche markets. They excel in the details that are so critical for that activity. I wouldn't want to distract them or change their approach," I cautioned.

"They take no risk and are short-sighted."

"Not exactly, but they don't need to take a lot of risk in those markets. Let the new trader handle the big international cargos in and out of the east."

"Paper trading is the best area to focus on. Lots of opportunity to grow."

"A bit, but I'm much more comfortable with the physical cargo movements built on relationships and cross-regional coordination than technical trading of paper. We've built a global cargo trading business to leverage here in the east."

This conversation stretched to the end of the day. But rather than a constructive tone, it felt abrasive and disrespectful. Dieter may have been right in some regards, and I tended to provide a lot of autonomy to my regional team leads, but his style sparked my defensive posture, which further deteriorated the conversation and my mindset. My bond with the longer-term staff and the preservation of team chemistry was also critical to me. Dieter's view was in stark contrast to the culture I sought to embed worldwide.

That night I pondered whether Dieter could be a "plant" into our LPG team from his previous manager, Nigel Foster.

He was very close to Nigel, so I had no doubts he often shared his LPG insights with him. I sensed Nigel always had an agenda to extend his Chemical Feedstocks remit into LPG, given common uses and markets. However, I convinced myself I was just being paranoid. Either way, I was not pleased with my change of leadership in Singapore.

I returned home on Friday and crashed from fatigue. I had one week in the office before the kids' February school break. After our initial visit to Israel the previous fall we immediately scheduled a return to see more sights and embrace the culture once again. We were headed back to Jerusalem in a week. It was truly a rat race. Non-stop business and family travel made for a surreal, amazing, and exhaustive expat experience.

On Monday, I headed into the office to catch up on paperwork and meet with my manager, Harold, to debrief him on my Singapore trip. Harold and I had a cold relationship. He was relatively new to trading but quickly understood that much larger books than LPG drove his product trading organization's success and certainly the resultant bonuses. He seemed to have plenty of time for the larger books, yet he deflected my efforts to initiate some rapport. I feared his opinion of me was derived from the other managers more so than my own performance or initiative. The reality was that although I wished Harold had developed his view of me directly, I'm not sure that it would have been too favorable. Though I always sought to extend a resilient, determined, and engaging face, I suspected a seasoned manager like Harold could see through my façade. Yes, I cranked out the work, improved our financial performance a bit, and traveled a lot to see team and customer alike, but my rapport with stakeholders was rigid and understandably would have raised some concern. Was I fooling anyone anymore?

So, when I arrived at Harold's office for our noon appointment, my agenda was to provide updates of my interviews for Singapore trading candidates and to review our Far East growth. I had prepared my approach during the flight back the previous week. However, as I kicked off Harold immediately interjected. "Steve, stop. I have something else I'd like to discuss. I've thought about the business a bit and…" he squirmed in his chair, shifting right, then left and staring at the floor. "I've decided to combine your LPG trading team with Nigel's Chemical Feedstocks team. Nigel will be the manager."

He looked up. He could see the shock on my face as he finished his assault with: "And your role will be eliminated." Harold paused, but seemed to smirk, noticeably pleased at relieving himself of his burden.

I had suspected my relationship with Harold and Nigel was not good. I had even become suspicious of Nigel's intentions. But I kept attributing those thoughts to paranoia and low self-esteem. I truly hadn't anticipated this bombshell. My mouth dropped and my eyes sank. I'm sure my face showed the disbelief and cycle of questions running through my mind.

After a long minute of shock and contemplation, I blurted out, "Wow! How long have you been considering this, Harold? I would have liked to have been involved in this."

My surprise quickly transitioned to anger. My voice rose an octave and cracked as I rattled off more questions in rapid succession: "Was Nigel involved in the decision? What's driving the decision? What about my team? What about me?"

Harold was not prepared to dive into the background or the answers. He looked down and then shot a glance at the clock, contemplating his escape. While his meandering attempt at consolation faded in my ears, I strained to organize my thoughts. "Harold, we are making big progress in LPG. We have restructured the team and upgraded the talent. We are making a dent in the global LPG market. I can understand the opportunity for greater synergies with Chem Feeds, but this sounds like an extreme change."

Harold retorted, "Nigel and I have discussed this for a while."

"I see…" I interjected, sending a cold stare straight at Harold.

"For a variety of reasons, we both feel this is the right thing to do. I know it's a lot to absorb. But you'll be ok. You plan to be on vacation next week, right?"

I wasn't sure if he was aiming for me to cancel my vacation, but I was determined not to acquiesce. "Yes, I'm on vacation next week. I would like to discuss this more before I leave. I'd like to understand your objectives and perhaps there are other ways to get there."

But Harold was not prepared to rehash any further. "The decision has been made, Steve. Relax. Have a good vacation. When you get back, I trust you will transition your items smoothly to Nigel."

Realizing there was no room for discussion I inquired, "So, what do I do next?"

"After transition, I have some projects for you to work on while you post for your next role in Shell. I'll help you with that." Anxious to close this contentious discussion, Harold got up and led me to the door as he headed to his next meeting.

And with that, my chapter as LPG trading leader was over.

I slowly walked back to my desk in a cloudy haze, just looking ahead, not daring to glance aside for fear I would see Nigel or others who might know. I lifelessly sank into my chair and stared blankly at Mike, sitting next to me. "Harold is combining LPG and Chem Feeds under Nigel."

Mike's head dropped. "Shit, I'm sorry about that." He sat still and silent.

I mumbled, "I've got to go." I grabbed my coat and headed out for a long walk on the streets of London. I'd never been in such a predicament. I sat on a frigid wrought iron bench in

Embankment Park starring at the London Eye across the River Thames. I was the only one brave enough—or numb enough—to withstand the frigid weather. My thoughts jumped from anger to confusion about how such a critical decision regarding my business and my team could have been made without me. Had they been scheming together? Was Nigel really as conniving as I had conjured up in my mind? Was Dieter part of this plan? Did he know what was going on while we debated last week? Even, Mike, my closest ally, was standoffish when I told him. Did he know what was going on while I was in Singapore?

As wet sleet started to fall, I got up to walk to Trafalgar Square. We were making progress in LPGs. What was wrong? Maybe I just pissed off too many people with the whirlwind staffing and strategy changes when I first arrived? I never really fit in socially with Harold and his other managers. Maybe I should have been part of the good ol' boy network? Maybe they saw through my façade at my strain and discomfort and felt it was not a good fit? Everyone could see I'd gained a lot of weight. Maybe stories of my drunken exploits in Singapore and London's South Bank got to Harold? After the fuel oil ethics issue in the States, maybe he felt he had to pull the plug? I was frustrated with so many looming questions. I pondered each as I slushed across the street.

Cold and wet, I climbed the steps to the National Gallery, my favorite art museum in London. As I entered, the warmth slid over me and the calmness of the first room's Italian Renaissance paintings slowed my heart. I sat to reflect what was next?

Damn! I'm going to be out of a job soon and I'm thousands of miles from home. What are my options?

My natural tendency was to put some structure around my predicament. As best I gleaned from Harold's words, I had some time to find another job—probably until the kids were done with school in June, at least. Though Shell rarely let people go, I had to assume I might not have a job after June and might even have to find my way back to the States without Shell. So I needed to touch base with my network of contacts in Houston. All I'd really known the last decade was trading. But from such a high post, could I find another job in trading? Was I now damaged goods in trading? What about roles outside of trading? Outside of Shell? So many things to consider. I knew I needed to get a list together and get to work. I certainly wasn't going to rely upon Harold to help me find another job, as he had intimated. It was time to pull myself together and take control. But first I needed to go home and talk to Jennifer. I grabbed my coat and headed to Waterloo to catch the train.

"Is everything okay?" Jennifer asked with a concerned look on her face. It was mid-afternoon, hours before I usually arrived.

"Rough day, Jennifer. Come here." I motioned her over as I slumped into the couch. "I had a meeting with Harold this morning to talk about my Singapore trip." The words slowly escaped my mouth. "I can't believe I'm saying this. He's combining my team with Nigel's and I'm out of a job in the spring."

Jennifer's face went white. But, true to form, she recovered quickly. She stood in front of me and bent over to give me a hug. "It'll be okay. We'll figure it out." She sat down next to me.

I ran through the indelible conversation with Harold. Jennifer listened and patted my knee. When I paused, she turned toward me, her face warmed up. "Steve, this is what we've been looking for! It's a chance to make the change. To get out of trading. To go home!"

Still weighed down by the days' events, I softly responded, "Well, I suppose so. Maybe... maybe this is good news. No more travel. No more late-night calls. But I have to find a job."

"You'll find something, Steve. Something better. I'm sure you will." We sat in silence, both pondering the challenges ahead. "I love you."

Suddenly, with a newfound air of optimism, I realized it was February 4th, 18 years to the day after Jennifer and I first met. "I love you too, honey."

The next day I rode the train in, rehashing the turn of events from the day before. I was still incensed at how Harold had arrived at his decision and puzzled at who else might have been involved. I'm usually not one to hold a grudge, but I hated Harold for what he was putting me through. The risk to my ability to provide for my family was petrifying. I was humiliated when I considered how my teammates and trading cohorts would react to my sudden demise. But as the train pulled into Waterloo I knew this was the best thing for me. I needed to hold my head high, share the news and my support, and get ready for the transition. I spent the rest of the week announcing the changes to my global team, preparing my résumé for my job search, and scheduling my first transition meeting with Nigel upon my return from vacation on February 18.

Needless to say, our one-week revisit to Israel was filled with lots of emotions, few of which had anything to do with the amazing scenes, history, or people surrounding us. I was nervous about the job search that lay ahead, and I was anxious to get started. At this point, it appeared my career in trading was over. It was all I'd known since returning from Detroit in 1996. My network was concentrated within trading. I was quite apprehensive. My stomach was tied in knots worrying about the social interactions and risk-taking required to cold call Shell managers back in Houston.

When I returned from vacation, I asked for more feedback from Harold, Nigel, and Harold's manager, Erwin Walters. But the story line came back much the same: "Just business, you'll be all right." However, their actions spoke louder than their words. After a two-hour transition meeting, Nigel professed to be ready and shoved me out posthaste. I bid a final farewell by phone to my globally scattered team and was left to my time-filler projects and, more importantly, my job search.

As I began to develop my list of job options, the silver lining became more apparent. I had suffered from a very bad work/life balance and the stress of the job had affected my health and marriage and thus change was critical. I'd known that since Hiroshima, if not before. Yet, I had not mustered up the courage to make the necessary change myself. In one 30-minute meeting, Harold had done that for me. I might never find out how or why this all took place, but I was now able to accelerate my personal time frame for a life correction by two years. My determination took over. It was time for this abusive chapter in my life to end.

Though many calls were odd, I introduced myself to new people and provided a plausible yet positive answer when some asked why I was searching for a new role. "My three-year expat assignment is nearly up so I'm looking for my next role back in the States." I've always found most Shell managers are so giving of their time for those seeking to network. Only in such situations did I realize the breadth of Shell's various commercial organizations. I talked to leaders in chemicals, gas trading, procurement, exploration and production, and midstream pipelines to name just a handful.

After cold-calling nearly 50 Shell managers, evaluating many roles, and posting on a few, I began to focus on a role as America's Gas Midstream Manager in Shell's growing upstream organization in Houston. The job would successfully detach me from the politics and friction within trading. Travel would be significantly less, limited primarily to New Orleans and Calgary. The manager was very engaging and excited to bring my commercial, operational, and team leadership experience to his group of scheduling and business development staff. I was officially offered the role on April 28, 2008. In my journal I wrote only: "Awesome. Hallelujah!"

I was so relieved this agonizing process was over. I could finally leave all this behind: the stress, the travel, the politics. Some work definitely lay ahead for me, but returning from the UK could provide such a reset.

SECTION FOUR – REFOCUS

CHAPTER 17: RESET

With our repatriation now imminent, we embarked on several short trips during our last month in Europe. In May we rented a barge for a weekend voyage on the River Thames. This majestic waterway flows through southern England easterly from quaint countryside villages past London before stretching out to the English Channel. After a brief training session, the family boarded near Windsor. We were our own captain and host for our two-day adventure. We steered the barge and, more critically, operated the many locks used to traverse the elevation changes of the storied river. After the stress of our last few years, not to mention the last few months battling the unknown, escaping into this gorgeous scenery of flowing hills and occasional castle towers was quite soothing. Despite a few bruises as the five of us managed several bumpy approaches and tie-ups to the narrow docks, we eventually glided into our evening stop. We brought Shabbat dinner on board, lighting the Sabbath candles enveloped by the darkness and peacefulness of our surroundings. We sang traditional Shabbat songs and played some board games, which provided us with the warmth of family that chilly spring night.

On Saturday, the kids reflected on their London experience and their excitement of returning home. Gwen had grown so much, becoming more communicative and active thanks to the proactive Portesbury teachers and our coaxing her through the streets of Europe. We treated her much like her sister and anyone else her age. She responded well and proved to be quite capable of keeping herself busy with music, dance, and art. At 13, she was prepared for middle school in Houston.

Madolyn, now 12, had perhaps the fullest European experience of the kids. Her mind and confidence expanded as she guided us through airports during our frequent travels. Madolyn and I began to have many grownup conversations about history, news, politics, and religion. She was curious and opinionated. She would join Gwen in seventh grade and welcomed a return to her childhood friends.

Noah was only six, but he had grown from a toddler peeing across Europe to a little boy making friends with his engaging smile and personality. Each of the kids was quite comfortable to travel and saw the world through a more diverse and appreciative lens.

Jennifer was stronger than ever, having raised three kids almost independently in a foreign land. With all our travels and her tens of thousands of pictures, she planned to explore a photography business upon our return.

On Sunday morning, we woke to an unexpected blanket of snow across the Thames. British weather was often gloomy and unpredictable. Yet for this last UK trip, nature was offering us a most splendid scene of light snow along the shorelines. We bundled up and pointed our barge east to return. We all took turns piloting the barge through the snow, taking pictures and marveling at our good fortunes on one of our favorite trips.

A few weeks later we headed off on our last family adventure. With only a long weekend school break we flew into Germany, rented a car, and drove to Saltzburg, Austria, for a tour of the *Sound of Music* scene. Afterwards we whisked away on a drive-by of Lichtenstein before spending a couple of days enjoying the beauty of the Swiss Alps and the tranquility of the posh yet meticulous nature of Lucerne and Zurich. Next, we wound our way through the dense German forests of Bavaria to our return flight. Hand-in-hand as we boarded the plane, Jennifer and I released deep sighs.

"Wow, our last mad dash trip. Ready to go home?" I asked.

"I'm so ready. But I will miss these family travels and my time with the kids," Jennifer offered. "I really got to know them these past few years. I feel closer than ever to each of them."

"Yeah, I can see that. I think that's great. I wish I'd had more of that experience. But I'm so happy you had each other." I paused. "Thanks for being there."

She patted my hand.

"I'm ready to go home," I exclaimed.

Finally, my last day in the office, June 3, 2008, arrived. Done with the entire office scene, I opted to step out and enjoy London one last time with an afternoon farewell tube tour on the Circle Line. I started at Embankment Station, wrapping through over a dozen stops. I was heading counterclockwise, literally unwinding along the journey.

I took a seat and cracked open my journal.

June 3, 2008 at 1:02 PM

I came to London and this job nervous and excited. I think the pressure of the role here at trading's head office must have gotten to me. Despite creating many social opportunities to get together, the rapport and teamsmanship with staff never replicated what we had in fuel oil. Perhaps some of that was due to cultural divides.

I glanced up as the train approached King's Cross station, where nearly three years ago a subway car left this very location before it was destroyed during the bombing of 7/7 in London. I then returned to my thoughts:

June 3, 2008 at 1:25 PM

But I never put the time in one-on-one. Maybe I felt I needed to move too fast. Was that driven by my boss or just my own unchecked determination? I think I was concerned that soliciting input of staff and colleagues would show weakness on my part. So I plowed ahead and changed our strategy, our staff, and our culture in a vacuum. The culture certainly changed, but not toward the tight-knit team I had envisioned. It took a long time for me to soften up and for staff to give me another chance to rebuild a bond. I never even put that effort in with the other product leaders. In retrospect, I could have gained a lot of insight into the global role, and it would have helped to have them in my corner. I'd certainly bitten off more than I could chew. This job may never have proven to be a good fit for a shy, introverted person like me, but my addictive behaviors which had helped push me out of my comfort zone in the past led me to bypass critical building blocks this time.

Baker Street, next stop, where in 2007 I'd started coming to a therapist every couple of weeks to gain some direction.

June 3, 2008 at 1:30pm

Those sessions helped me recognize that much of the pressure I felt came from me. I needed to be kinder to myself and take control of my choices. Though this opened my eyes, the stressful work situations were coming fast and furious and I just couldn't get in front of them at the time.

As the train soon approached High Street Kensington, I shoved the journal into my bag and exited the tube. Three years ago, we'd moved to our corporate apartment on this street. We were so excited and had such grand expectations of our time together. Walking down the street, I caught an image in a shop window. Wow, was that me? I looked like crap. I was 40 pounds heavier. My hair was receding and graying, and my face carried the strain from the lines across my forehead to the drooping cheeks and triple chin. *I really did a number on myself,* I thought. I knew it was not healthy that one person must handle so much stress. I further realized that alleviating such stress by diving into Ben & Jerry's Phish Food, a McDonald's #3 meal, or vodka and tonics was not helping the matter. My body understood that and reacted by turning my nose into a red beacon only Rudolph would have been proud of—not to mention my ordeal with sciatica, shingles, and other self-inflicted stress signals, all of which just increased the very strain I needed to minimize.

My drinking was clearly my roughest edge. I had blackouts, got lost, and had some stupid, dangerous escapades. It calmed my fears for a few hours here and there, but at what cost? Like the time I was chauffeuring friends in Houston in 1989, I felt the creation of these drinking experiences would entice the team to like me. But these were generally business relationships—temporary and superficial. I had abused my authority in order to entice them to join in my social sphere, a form of coping mechanism for me. Yet as I departed they moved on, and I was left with a lot of scars to heal.

As I sat on a bench at Holland Park, where my kids had played in those early days in London, I wondered...

June 3, 2008 at 2:32 PM

Am I an alcoholic? It's hard for me to classify my drinking problem. I wasn't drinking every day or even most days. I wasn't drinking alone either... just in social situations, where I knew no bounds. Terming it as alcoholism seemed to discount those times and make them part of a disease. It also implied that to truly conquer my problem I must stop drinking altogether, a concept that made me shudder. I just didn't have the courage to wage that battle yet. A battle that if won, would strip away the coping mechanism I feared I might still need to live happily with my introverted personality and social anxiety. Yet life had to be different when we returned. Stressful or not, I couldn't eat and drink my way through another job. Everything needed to change: the city, the job, the team. I needed to change.

Back on the tube headed to Embankment, I stared at a picture of Jennifer tucked in my journal.

June 3, 2008 at 3:07 PM

I caused her such pain. With her help and my own maturity, I must find the moderation—with my drinking, eating, and work/life balance—that I need, and my family deserves.

As my Circle Line tube returned to Embankment and I walked across the bridge for my last South West Train from Waterloo, I was finally ready to put this episode in the rearview mirror and return to Houston for a reset. For the last time on the train, I scribbled in my journal:

June 3, 2008 at 3:22 PM

So many leadership lessons: patience, networking with peers, seeking counsel, balancing confidence and humility through compromise. Ready for a new chapter.

I closed my book and dozed off.

CHAPTER 18: TIGHT GENES

Transitions are never easy. The kids' American School even provided classes to help those families preparing to repatriate to the States each summer. We were returning to the same neighborhood and friends we'd left three years earlier, but with stories of Sabbath in Jerusalem, snow on the Thames, and croissants at the Eiffel Tower. So we left excited, but a bit anxious about the adjustment that lay ahead.

As challenging as the London work had been, my struggles with the choices laid out at Hiroshima and the nature of the cold conclusion to my assignment the past winter all helped me to learn and grow. With my share of sulking and anger behind me, I realized the opportunity placed before me. It was time to use my newfound lessons and put health and family first. I had lots of work to do.

My poor health, and my weight in particular, had been an issue for decades. But the tinderbox I'd occupied for the past few years had taken a big toll. For me, eating had always been a prevalent issue serving a purpose not only to cope with stressful situations, but also to celebrate the relief of the completion of such times. Whether I had just completed a presentation, a cocktail hour, or a tough, three-year assignment in London, I fell to temptation and gorged myself.

With such relief and return to the familiar places and eateries in Houston, I went on a variety of self-indulging binges. At work, my floor's vending machine seemed to know my name. However, several times I walked from one end of the sprawling work campus to the other to find a newly stocked dispensary to stuff a couple of chocolate muffins and a pack of Twix bars in my face. With increased food intake, I was going to the bathroom so much I nearly set up a workstation in stall number three. It was an ongoing battle I was far from winning.

I had logged many diets as an adult; some resulting in as much as 20- to 50-pound weight loss. I tried Weight Watchers, carb-free diets, chicken-only regimens, and a variety of diet pills with varying success. However, any determination and victory down this roller coaster always ended up in a soaring climb beyond my original weight when the obsessive effort of counting calories and banishing foods became overwhelming.

Eventually, such extreme behavior shifted the other way, inviting private binging on chocolate, carbs, and fast food. I would devour a few doughnuts en route to work, only to follow up with breakfast upon arrival. Later, I would grab several snacks when topping up the car with gas and then hit drive-thru restaurants on the way home for dinner. I made sure to bury any wrappers deep in the trashcan when I got home to protect my secret. I couldn't get enough, and it showed. I was putting on five pounds a month!

Jennifer continued to be my rock and inspiration in my health journey. "You can do it, Steve. I know it's not easy, but I want to help."

She prepared many healthy meals at night. Yet, she only knew the half of it, as I was too embarrassed to share the extreme gorging I had fallen prey to lately.

The roller coaster ride was worse than anything. I considered ending the struggle and relinquishing myself to obesity. Maybe I would be happier? Maybe that was truly who I was? But the fact was I wasn't healthy at 5'6" and 255 pounds. It was becoming dangerous. Additionally, my self-esteem found new depths at such weight. Given that eating was one of my major coping mechanisms for stress, any nonchalant path was sure to land me at 300 pounds before too long. I didn't look good, generally didn't feel good, and probably hadn't attracted Jennifer's goggling eyes in years. I kept looking for the grand epiphany, but past signs or doctor's coaxing had only provided temporary motivation at best. Must I wait for a heart attack?

Meanwhile in late 2008, determined to invoke a family-first approach, we drove to Birmingham to rekindle our traditional Friedman family Thanksgiving. After about 20 of us enjoyed plenty of catching up, feasting on all the traditional foods, playing our time-honored kickball game, and cheering Alabama to a 36-0 shellacking of Auburn, we embarked on our 13-hour drive back to Houston. Midway through Mississippi, my right leg began throbbing. I tended to do most of the driving, so I assumed I just needed a break. After nursing my discomfort the rest of the day, we finally arrived home safely. I expected my leg would benefit from some wraps and relaxation, but the pain did not subside.

A few days later I visited my doctor who was alarmed at my story. He noticed my right calf was considerably larger than my left. Suspecting I had deep vein thrombosis (DVT) or a blood clot, he sent me to the hospital for an immediate ultrasound. After his diagnosis was confirmed, he put me on blood thinners to break apart the clot. My doctor also ran some tests and determined I had a genetic predisposition for blood clotting, a condition called Prothrombin mutation. Though I had no previous clotting history, it was possible that unprovoked clots could form in my calf or, worse yet, in my thigh or lungs where they could move to the brain and cause strokes or even death. Yet remaining on blood thinners carried the risk of bleeding out in the case of bruises or cuts, as clotting or simple scabbing could become less likely. Thus, after my clot disappeared, the doctor and I discussed the risks of an ongoing blood thinner routine and decided I should just take breaks during long travels and monitor my condition. Finally, he echoed what I'd heard from doctors for years: "Lose weight."

This time, those words rippled throughout my life. I needed to address the source of my weight gain: the strain I placed on myself. Thankfully, as my escape from trading was complete and the stressful transition into my new team eased, my skin rashes began to dissipate. It was amazing how reduced stress and a more balanced lifestyle were reflected by the body. Now I needed to figure out how to tackle my weight problem. However, my body was not done talking to me.

The following year, I began to feel some discomfort around my mid-section. I attributed it to a bad stomachache and some mild, recurring back aches. However, when it didn't cure itself, I visited my primary doctor once again. I expected my diagnosis to be confirmed, but to his credit the doctor ran several tests and ultimately determined I had yet another genetic marker.

Ironically (pun intended), I found that I was afflicted with hemochromatosis, a genetic predisposition for retaining ferritin, or blood cells that contain iron. My doctor explained that hemochromatosis typically goes undetected for years. Though it was easy to test for and could be corrected, if left undiagnosed hemochromatosis could be fatal. I wanted to attribute some of my childhood liver dinners to my newly discovered condition, but there was no medical proof from which I could pin such guilt on my parents.

I also learned that people with hemochromatosis may show some or all of the most common symptoms including fatigue, bronzing of the skin, weight loss (or gain), pain in or around the liver, depression, arthritis, or hair loss. I could certainly claim some of these ailments. The doctor underscored how critical a healthy liver was, given its performance as the body's primary filter. Hemochromatosis can become dangerous at any stage in life, depending on the body's rate of accumulating excess iron since birth. If it goes undetected, the extra iron/ferritin, which builds up can deposit in the liver or other organs, eventually resulting in "rusting from within." That sounded very scary.

Once I was diagnosed through a full iron panel and genetic testing, it was determined my ferritin level was 1,486 PPM, well over the 100-200 PPM norm. This drove my doctor to order a liver culture to determine if I had any scarring of my liver. Though the hole-punch biopsy indicated the hemochromatosis had been caught in time, my doctor did use the opportunity to sternly counsel me that my liver was not healthy. My biopsy indicated dangerous enzyme levels, prompted by a 40% fat composition. My weight was a big factor. My red meat-based diet, my history of alcohol consumption, and my guzzling of NutraSweet-laden diet sodas all raised my risk of future damage and hence the likelihood of needing a liver transplant in the relatively near future. Losing weight was no longer optional.

In the meantime, my high ferritin count was corrected by months of weekly phlebotomies; i.e., donating a pint of blood until enough of my old, ferritin-laden blood was removed. After that, quarterly phlebotomies were prescribed to continue to maintain satisfactory levels. The removed blood could not be donated but had to be thrown away, given the toxicity of the ferritin levels.

This became a catalyst for me to eliminate red meat and any alcohol for over a year, and after that to consume only in moderation. I was also instructed to stop drinking any diet sodas as the filtering of the NutraSweet chemicals was quite taxing on my liver. It was time to start listening to my doctors and my own conscience and begin a regimen to lose weight fast.

While my propensity for both blood clotting and ferritin retention were genetic, my lifestyle was of my own choosing. My doctors now considered my health "dangerous." I suppose that was what I deserved after so many years abusing my body.

After these diagnoses, I had fits of self-pity. Why me? After my London experience, what other curve balls must I deal with? But at least I was now aware of these risks. I had to own my mistakes—all of them. Though I often recognized past forks in the road at storied locales like Hiroshima and Prague, I always seemed to lack the mettle to pursue the right path with vigor. Now, in Houston, I was presented with another critical test of courage and determination.

CHAPTER 19: MORE ENERGY

My move to midstream provided an interesting transition from trading to Shell's upstream organization, which focused on exploring, producing, and transporting crude oil and natural gas. Once I made this transition, I reflected upon the unique culture of Shell's trading organization, which I'd been a part of for 12 years. Trading maintained an aura of superiority and glamour that was further inflated by the bigger bonus program necessary to attract and maintain the best staff in this very competitive part of the industry. Social events like dinners, drinks, golf, and fishing were much more common in trading than within the rest of Shell, given the focus on growing external relations and commercial deal-making. Moving from such an environment, which was relished by many but merely endured by introverts like me, was a catalyst to reevaluate my strengths and ambitions.

Throughout Shell we branded personnel with a forecast capability, a label intended to reflect management's view of how far an individual might advance in the organization. While the process was less than perfect and tended to make employees feel like their fate was predetermined, it did help the company to plan resources and supervisors to have productive discussions with staff regarding gaps that must be addressed in order to promote future development.

Staff capability was assessed based on three key principles aligned with **Accomplishment**, **Intelligence**, and **Engagement**.

Accomplishment: Given my task and goal-oriented approach, I always excelled in accomplishment. My work ethic and personal drive consistently ensured I delivered more than expected, and this didn't go unnoticed.

Intelligence: While I certainly had "smarts," I never considered myself to be an "intellectual" by any means. This was generally okay, as most jobs were not overly complex. In my later and more advanced roles, I admittedly felt frustrated by some financial models and advanced exposure management techniques. Dare I say I was not alone in this area, but it signaled an intelligence ceiling which I recognized at the time.

Engagement: The engagement pillar was always an interesting assessment. My true introverted nature surely influenced a lower score. However, my compulsive initiative to achieve and my ability to tackle social tasks while masking the stress that it caused me branded my engagement skills at least at a threshold level.

In combination with intelligence and accomplishment, my engagement score provided an assessment commensurate with senior management level. This supported a strong résumé and provided reassurance of my skills and Shell's recognition of my capabilities that had paved a path full of promotions earlier in my career.

However, during my management progression, I acknowledged my intelligence limitations and the personal stress which the engagement aspect had placed on me. As I reflected on my career and lessons learned after London, I suspected I would fall short of my predetermined senior management assessment. That was not such an easy thing to admit, having grown up in a corporate world expecting unending ambition and advancement. Anything less could be viewed as a weakness, a stalled career, and even expendability. I was always conscious of this risk, since job security was paramount for me.

If nothing else, my career thus far had taught me I was not good at the "fake it 'til you make it" approach. Perhaps I was fooling some or many, but certainly not everyone. Besides, my attempt to create this façade was too draining and stressful. If this was what Shell's promotion track looked like, I needed to get off the train. I learned that success at any cost was too high a price for me.

My tumultuous term in London convinced me life balance, health and happiness were most important. I was finally ready to put work into the proper perspective and make the dramatic changes to refocus my life.

Thus, I shifted my ambitions from a title (Senior Leader) to a purpose—one that utilized my strengths for team building and mentoring while managing within an acceptable level of personal anxiety. A middle management position with a small local team of commercial and operations staff could be my sweet spot.

Hence, midstream became the perfect landing place. It brought me back to Houston and provided a long overdue exit from trading. From the start, I enjoyed the support of the hiring manager and my predecessor, Marcus Pearlman. He took a chance on me—someone he did not know, who was new to the midstream business, and whom he could only interview by phone for such an important job. The role was very attractive from a business growth and team leadership perspective. The focus on commercial and scheduling tasks was similar to my earlier roles. After the turmoil in London, the organizational culture and rapport with Marcus felt like a safe place to recover, practice what I'd learning, and enjoy a less stressful life for myself and my family.

The gas midstream team consisted of about a dozen commercial business development managers and gas schedulers located in Houston and Calgary. Each commercial manager worked on maintaining existing contracts and relationships and negotiated new arrangements to transport Shell's natural gas from production sites to trading and storage markets. This might include renting space on existing pipelines or enlisting capacity in new-build pipes. Our areas of operation ranged from the deep waters of the Gulf of Mexico to onshore production in western Canada. The commercial team also managed gas processing plant agreements where raw natural gas was split into its components: natural gas and my previous stomping ground of LPGs. Our gas schedulers managed every movement, coordinating with the production facilities, various pipe and plant providers, and ultimately with our customers who bought the gas at market. My new role was to supervise all staff, provide commercial and strategic guidance to the team, and communicate with my management, peers, and industry counterparts.

Rather than steamroll over most workers with my own vision or use alcohol to build relationship as I'd done in London, I wanted to now work closely with staff to help them identify and cultivate their own strengths and pursue exciting career paths. Maybe I was drawn to this to make amends for my past sins, but I found this new approach exciting and gratifying. Hence, during my tenure I began to challenge the traditional Shell approach, which focused on shoring up perceived weaknesses through an inordinate amount of training and coaching. I wanted to do something different. I adopted the mantra that it was best to focus on developing and leveraging peoples' strengths—both my own and each team member's as well.

Rather than sending staff to classes to address shortcomings (classes they loathed and probably cursed me for in the past), now we were developing new tools to enhance strengths that could expand our performance and delivery exponentially.

Providing new negotiating tips for those most excited about commercial performance or exposing operations staff to field locations and critical processes in order to build such expertise could be both powerful and motivational.

Furthermore, to assess each team member's passion and adjust work tasks to take advantage of such group dynamics could help develop a more cohesive and progressive culture. These changes didn't happen easily or quickly, either in myself or within our midstream team. It took patience and sensitivity to recognize where each staff member might be on this change journey. But it was an exciting venture that replaced much of my supervisory stress with satisfaction.

I, too, was prepared to change—to try to accept my own reserved, introspective, and somewhat compulsively structured personality as a strength. Thus, I chose to leverage my project management skills to schedule many engagements from the beginning. This enabled me to use my mentoring skills to establish strong foundations, especially with younger staff. Critically, I would now hire with the objective to build a complete team, surrounding myself with trustworthy people that could provide both challenge and support, as well as fill my stylistic gaps. I wanted to ensure I could lean on some staff who excelled at stakeholder management and those who possessed the necessary technical skills which I lacked.

This job also gave me the chance to stay in role longer than my standard two or three years. A longer tenure would provide the opportunity to build deeper roots within the team and industry. It would also give me a chance to maintain the organizational and cultural changes I implemented. While shorter tenures often led to faster promotions, each transition carried a new level of stress, which had become exhausting.

When I arrived in midstream in mid-2008, Shell and the industry had made significant technical advances that sparked a new North American expansion into previously uneconomical onshore locations. Shell aimed to leverage its formative Gulf of Mexico experience, technical leadership, and deep pockets to become a top quartile producer in the North American onshore markets. Midstream was gearing up to support this challenge in over a dozen new basins across North America. It presented exciting opportunities.

Unfortunately, only a few months after my arrival the US economy plummeted into recession in August 2008. Natural gas prices dove from nearly $13 per unit, eventually falling below $3. This certainly gave the team cause for concern. However, convinced the onshore market was the future for US exploration and production, the industry continued to expand, keeping our midstream group extremely busy determining how to transport new, remote natural gas to market.

The gas midstream team was largely filled with very experienced "gray hairs." I harkened back to my Detroit days and the importance of learning and offering respect for such expertise. This time, I stretched myself to gain knowledge and support. Growth in the business allowed me to hire some new staff with less experience but broader, more diverse perspectives. Thus, we achieved a better balance within the team. Slowly, we instilled changes and built for the future. I relied upon the veteran team members to convey their expertise and our new staff to bring curiosity and energy alongside. Thus, each person had his/her role and we avoided the micromanaging that pervades many teams.

Though a friendly group, evening socials were not the norm. Most had long commutes at the end of the day and were satisfied to huddle over lunch every once in a while. Given I was not only determined to adhere to my doctor's health warnings, but also to my promise to put binge-drinking in my past, this team's culture helped remove any temptations. I actually found such an adjustment quite easy. I didn't miss the drinking but, to the contrary, was relieved that the pressure and risks to both my health and my relationships were gone. I reconciled that my excessive drinking over the past decade was not alcoholism, by definition, but extreme social drinking triggered by the intense strain built up around me. My new job brought a change of scenery and a new personal mindset that finally let me manage any challenges in a much healthier way.

I needed to establish this team through hard work and engagements rather than relying on my old habits. It required a sober approach. Only then could I make the best leadership decisions and initiate adjustments that had the best chance to provide a lasting, positive impact. It was not easy for me to change my style, but renewed confidence in my people-centered approach and the overwhelming support of my manager and staff paved the path.

Though my long hours in the office and at home were only somewhat moderated, it was now a labor of love. I enjoyed the challenge again and the opportunity to cultivate a team that could exceed everyone's expectations. Now, finally, I could stop swimming upstream and thrive.

CHAPTER 20: AFTERGLOW

As my new leadership style took hold and my confidence at work returned, I discovered a clear personal purpose and a newfound level of my own acceptance. I was not perfect—far from it. But I was a good person and I was determined to address my priorities to become the man I knew I could be. It had to start with my own health. I could not be the leader at work, not to mention the husband and father I wanted to be at home, until I took care of myself. According to my doctors, the best thing I could do for my hemochromatosis and blood-clotting risk was to get healthy—eat right and exercise. They placed no limitations on my activity, so I set off to explore Shell's on-campus gym. It was fully decked-out with plenty of weights and cardio machines and, most importantly, it was only a two-minute walk from the office.

As with most fitness facilities, our gym had a mix of members. A few diehards pushing the limit from the start, others just using the time for a light stroll to catch up on news or videos, and some crawling at such a pace they couldn't possibly break a sweat in 30 minutes. I like a pretty hard workout—I'd say 8 out of 10—and I like to finish dripping with sweat. I feel like I've accomplished something if I'm wringing out my shirt afterward before enjoying a nice cool shower.

A bit lost in my exercise after-glow as I waited in a long line for a shower stall to open up one day, I quipped, "perhaps we should double up," to make the line move faster. After a few odd stares and some additional line spacing, I realized my faux pas. Oh well, no harm. After my shower I had to shroud myself in such a short, Clorox-infused crunchy towel that could have left me with paper cuts, I had to submit a comment card: "The towels should be softer, and bigger. If I could actually stretch that puny towel around me, I wouldn't need to come to the gym in the first place." Nevertheless, the daily gym session served its purpose.

Many fitness experts have stated that the key to losing weight is controlled food intake more so than exercise, but I do find they are complementary. It's like a partnership, and if I stop one, the other fades in short order. Once I established my gym habit, I was able to stabilize my weight—albeit at a rotund 240 pounds—by late 2008. Nevertheless, I had a renewed sense of progress and accomplishment.

Next, the most essential area of focus for me was family. Though global travel was great, my family had suffered most from my long European workdays and trips, and the repercussions of the stress that ensued. Back home in Houston, I was able to attend school activities and join family dinners. The tension around the house relaxed, and I enjoyed sharing warm moments with everyone.

Only a few months after our return we were greeted by Hurricane Ike, which forced us to spend a night in our small pantry as tornados whirled around our neighborhood. Though our home was spared the destruction, power lines were snapped across the city. Thus, we then had to adapt to life without electricity, school, or running water for nearly three weeks. This was especially upsetting for Gwen who, preferring status quo and being very empathetic to other's pain, became concerned about other weather disturbances. However, once the power was restored, Gwen slowly returned to her routines and confidence.

There's no better way to demonstrate Gwen's confidence than through her wardrobe and her love of music. She wore what she liked (including a Hannah Montana wig, long sleeves, a skirt over her long pants, and mixed socks under her patent leather fancy shoes with her name labels on the front—all in late July) because, well, she wanted to do so. When she was *really* in her zone, she showed it with unabashed glee. Whether at a Miley Cyrus or Katy Perry concert or talking about her boyfriends and their "plans," her face showed such happiness that I didn't think anyone could beat her wide smile and rosy cheeks. She sang at the top of her lungs because she loved singing. She danced with such wild abandon—including spinning on the floor at the airport—because she could. Gwen was so free and uninhibited. Perhaps because of her Down syndrome maybe she knew no other way. Yet she is who she is and takes immense pride in that.

Gwen thrived back in Houston. She had learned to read and developed basic math skills in the UK. However, at times, she lamented some activities—like driving—which she expected she would never achieve. Yet she became determined to be more independent like her siblings. Now, instead of Jennifer or myself joining her at parties or social events, she kicked us to the curb, insisting we drop her off. She deflected being called a "kid" and wanted to make her own decisions. Jennifer and I supported her newfound goals of independence and encouraged her to share more of her day around the dinner table.

However, Gwen was like many kids—I mean young adults. She was not a big talker when it came to reporting on her day at school. So, at the dinner table I continued to ask: "How was school? Anything exciting? What did you do in math? How are your boyfriends?" Frustrated by my questions and unmoved by my pleading for a little peek into the day of a young student, she proceeded to the kitchen drawer, grabbed a roll of Scotch tape, and then liberally applied it, wrapping tape around my head and covering my mouth at least 10 times. Madolyn and Noah cheered as Gwen took matters into her own hands and did what the others had, assuredly, only wished they could do. When the inquisition was over, I had learned my lesson.

Meanwhile, sister Madolyn had grown up quite a bit in England, embracing the cultural experience and enduring the personal struggles to make friends in a transitory place. In many ways our return home felt seamless, yet the three-year experience abroad was certainly life-changing. Madolyn had matured and become more independent herself. She was creative, determined, and humble. A year after our return, she became a bat mitzvah along with Gwen. Madolyn carried most of the service but was happy to share the stage and accolades with her sister. Madolyn performed so beautifully— all the more remarkable, given her earlier diagnosis of dyslexia, which made learning and reading English, let alone Hebrew, quite challenging. Yet she persevered, largely teaching herself using musical scales and memorization.

During middle school Madolyn rekindled friendships and embraced the joys of local teenage theatre at the Jewish Community Center. She had fun with musicals, dancing, and the camaraderie of the community. As she aged out of the actor's group, she fell in love with the backstage. She began helping the director out as a stage management intern, planning every step and move of the show and making sure it ran smoothly. She eventually parlayed this into a paid position, all on her own.

In 2012, Madolyn got her driver's license and invited Gwen along for her first jaunt. I think Gwen was more excited than Madolyn. Gwen jumped into the passenger seat and unrolled her window as they backed out of the driveway. Exerting her independence as they drove away, Gwen threw her arms up and out the window, and yelled to Jennifer and me, "See ya, losers!" I doubled over in laughter as Thelma and Louise took off on their new adventure together.

Since returning, Noah blossomed from a cute little six-year-old with a slight British accent into a talented, confident young man. Noah was always very studious, curious, and principled. He took a lot of pride in his schoolwork and in following most every rule at school, at home, and in society in general—except, perhaps, those of etiquette. He still held on to his childhood and the chuckles he received when he displayed how he could burp the alphabet or share the stinkiest fart.

Seeking more publicly suitable hobbies, Noah tried gymnastics, karate, and even soccer, until finding his passion in music. By age eight Noah began singing in school choir and later the regional choir and Houston Boy Choir, a prestigious ensemble for young men. A few years later Noah picked up the piano. When he was home, he was often singing and sight-reading on the piano with such grace it brought back memories of my childhood home.

Noah had always been ambitious and independent in his own way. He had planned his own birthday parties since he was ten, tracked some company stocks, and learned website coding on his own. He was a sponge for new information. He asked *lots* of questions of me and his mom, of his teachers, and of any technical help desk with whom he would intelligently converse, sometimes for hours. If not for his high-pitched tone, they would have mistaken him for the adult in the family. Noah would fix our TV, phone, and Internet, and schedule callouts if he needed the experts on-site. While at camp one summer, he asked us to video the Best Buy installation of our new TV so he could see what they were doing.

In the meantime, Jennifer embraced our return to Houston as well. Her artistic calling shifted from scrapbooking to photography and genealogy. She captured the memories of a friend's wedding while uncovering trees of our ancestry dating back to 19th century Europe. True to her own reserved yet creative nature, Jennifer rekindled friendships while focusing most of her time raising our kids in such a tender way.

I was still taking my work home, both physically and mentally, but the stress level was much less than in trading. Thus, Jennifer and I shared more together, returning our relationship to one of trust and friendship that our marriage had been founded on decades earlier.

I used to consider my family time an escape from the chaos and repercussions of work. I was always so fortunate to have such a sanctuary. That comfort enabled me to wind down and remove my mask at night. Now that work was more enjoyable and my health was on the right track, family time elevated to an even higher calling, a peaceful time in which I could truly be myself with the people I loved the very most.

Perhaps I was no longer "faking it" at work, but I was certainly embracing my true self through the loving moments we shared as a family.

I've always enjoyed (and I think excelled) at the art of funny faces. I undoubtedly received this talent from my dad who managed to twist his mouth into some diagonals that always made me laugh. Now this skill was passing down to my kids, especially Madolyn, while Noah was still developing his facial plasticity.

These faces did come at a cost as Jennifer typically sought to capture a moment with a proper photo, though I believe she was just grateful to get one good picture before the contortion artistry began to take hold. These moments with the kids made me so proud. Mom used to say, "If you do that too much, your face might stay that way!" But so far, I respectfully disagree.

We celebrated all our holidays together. Passover and Thanksgiving were still my favorite family times, but

Halloween always reserved a special place in my heart. Some people love Halloween so much they decorate their yard, build spooky haunted tours through their house, and create the most elaborate costumes. I can't say I went to those extremes, but I did enjoy a good Tootsie Roll and a walk around the neighborhood. Over the years, I've managed to assemble a few unforgettable costumes, starting with my most memorable and perhaps most disturbing—that of a sperm—with my friend Ricky at the University of Alabama. A combination of latex, hose, makeup, and a fishy-type swimming motion grabbed the first place prize at a campus Halloween party.

From there, it could only go up(stream). In the early '90's I was a 'Bama elephant, complete with tons of gray makeup and a winning elephant call that could really pack (o-derm) a punch. Later I donned a cow uniform, which was moo-ving but particularly memorable as Madolyn (age two at the time) found my udders especially fun to play with, perhaps conjuring up some happy memories. Finally, in the 2000's I assembled a last-minute costume from the closet: "Backward Man." My clothes, hat, and glasses were all worn facing the back and I walked backward with a little help from the family. It was unique, but as I learned later, walking backward all night was a reversal of fortunes since I couldn't see to pick out the Tootsie Rolls from the neighbors' bags of treats.

While my past habits had taken many destructive forms, perhaps the oddest application was my affinity for chewing gum. I've always enjoyed a stick of gum, but it eventually became a bit of an obsession. Outside of work, I typically was chomping away at two or three sticks at any given time, usually rotating out amongst my favorite few minty or fruity options every 15 minutes or so. It's a wonder I didn't have bulging jaw muscles those days.

One night I placed my used gum in a dish that had thankfully replaced my Blackberry next to my bed. Within a few weeks, the dish was full and started to grow into a gum tree. Eventually, the dish was filled with hundreds of wads of chewed gum. Amazingly, that gum maintained its texture and smell. It was sort of like a scratch-and-sniff. The tree eventually maxed out, having lost its stability and fell, affixing to whatever it landed on. My dentist warned me of impending lockjaw. I hadn't thought about that. I'll have to chew on that possibility a little longer.

Returning to Houston enabled us to reacquaint with our extended family, primarily mine in Birmingham and Jennifer's in Kansas City. Growing up in Alabama, my favorite food staple was barbeque. Ribs smothered in sweet, thick sauce— mmm! I frequented Demetri's and Golden Rule until I went to school in Tuscaloosa and discovered Dreamland BBQ. Ribs, only ribs! Delicious meaty ribs! Even going there with my sister and watching her friend try to eat the ribs with fork and knife did not deter me from dreaming of Dreamland.

But once Jennifer introduced me to the Kansas City barbeque scene, I expanded my palate. Why hadn't burnt ends found their way out of KC and onto the national scene? What other cuts of the cow was I missing? That stuff was like heaven swimming in sauce. When we returned to Kansas City to see Auntie M and others, our favorite KC eatery was Jack Stack. As was typical, we tended to eat more than our fill. After one such visit, Madolyn and I crafted a top 10 list of reasons "Why Not to Go To Jack Stack Anymore" while on our flight home. Our favorites were "I have pieces of leather in between my teeth," "I have grown a second stomach and now I am chewing my cud," and "I just laid a load of cow patty in the aisle and it's swarming with flies." We were uncontrollably laughing to curious on-lookers around row 24.

Spending time with family was so fulfilling. Doing so with work being a bright glow in my life rather than an ominous shadow made all the difference.

CHAPTER 21: OPTIMAL

Happiness at home and work made it easier for me to continue to focus on my health. After years of a consistent if not monotonous gym routine, I was ready to bring my workouts and my fitness to a new level. The vehicle for such a leap was a reach back to my childhood.

Winters are not so tough in Houston, but given the stifling heat of summer, when spring arrives it's best to go out and enjoy the mild temperatures and relatively low humidity. It was just such a day in April 2011 when Jennifer convinced me that we should buy bicycles so the whole family could go on neighborhood rides. Bicycling was so relaxing and fun throughout my youth. Roger and I used to cruise the neighborhood and later I would find my own tranquility pedaling the hills for hours on a Saturday afternoon. I really hadn't ridden since I was in college, almost 25 years earlier.

That weekend we purchased a couple of bikes to join our kids cruising around the streets, waving at neighbors, gliding around corners and in and out of driveways. I felt like I was 11 again. The kids were enjoying the break from their phones and TV, while unwittingly appreciating a gentle introduction into exercise and relaxation at the same time. We finished our first neighborhood tour, promising to return at least weekly. However, conflicting schedules, the rush of life, and the abhorrent heat and humidity of summertime made such a commitment hard to fulfill.

But that first bike ride lit a spark in me. I felt a sense of calmness that I craved. I wanted to explore it further. I needed to! So, a couple of weekends later I hopped on my hybrid bike at 7 AM on a Saturday and rode about 15 miles. Peace, serenity, solitude. This was different from the tranquility I craved previously. While in LPGs I needed the time for a walk in London during lunch or a weekend foray in Hiroshima to balance the strain of a life turned upside down. Now, the serenity just helped me reflect and think. It was no longer a solitude of desperation but one of inner joy.

Naturally, my addictive behavior fueled my cycling and I craved more. I wanted to explore, to go further, faster. Within a few months, in the draining heat of the Houston summer, I eventually stretched my 15-mile trip to 70-mile Saturday morning excursions across the city to Hobby Airport, the San Jacinto Monument, and to neighboring cities like Sugar Land. My pace picked up and I learned a lot about riding: the safety aspects, proper gear, the importance of hydrating and refueling, and how to outrun dogs with an adrenalin-induced full-out sprint. For a non-athletic person, I was quite proud of my accomplishments, and I was finally losing weight and getting fit.

Initially, my weekend rides didn't distract from family time, but were actually a critical part of my family-first approach. I needed the introspective time and improved health to continue to grow as a productive member of the family. Besides, my 6 AM departures ensured I was back from most of my rides by 11 AM, before the kids were even up from their weekend slumber.

Noah asked, "How could you bike for hours on the road? Aren't you bored?" But I rarely was. I especially enjoyed the solitude biking offered: thinking time to ponder work and family items, to prepare for big work projects, to sort out issues I couldn't figure out during the week. Only after hours of biking did I return to reality, as I did on my longest trek when I was 40 miles from home at Bush Intercontinental Airport. Staring through a fence down a busy runway, I suddenly realized I was exhausted and drained, the energy to concentrate on self-therapy gone, and I was still 40 miles, or about three hours, from home. This time I had finally pushed myself too far. But I was not prepared to accept defeat and climbed on my bike for a grueling ride home. I made it back by mid-afternoon and slept the rest of the day.

In the fall, someone suggested I should sign up for the BP MS 150, a two-day bike ride sponsored by the energy giant, benefiting multiple sclerosis. The ride involved cycling from Houston to Austin over two days, covering about 170 miles in total. This challenge, one that surely required training and focus, was the motivation I needed to continue to raise the bar. I signed up and then entered the Conoco Training Series that kicked off in January 2012.

I nicknamed my bike Steel Horse after a line in Bon Jovi's hit "Wanted Dead or Alive," given it was considerably heavier than most of the other road bikes. I went on organized rides every other weekend, and local jaunts on my own the other Saturdays. The training progressed from 25 miles to 75 miles, from flat to very hilly by Texas standards, while sometimes battling stiff 20 mph winds. The training series helped me step up my game physically, but it especially challenged me mentally. Fighting the elements and completing every ride boosted my confidence. Cycling with hundreds and sometimes thousands of other riders presented a steep learning curve. Not only did I have to be more conscious of spacing, but I also had to fight my competitive nature to try to outrun others and refocused on my own objectives.

Despite losing almost 50 pounds, I was still over 200. My husky physique, along with my heavy sit-up style hybrid bike made outrunning more fit riders on their feather-light titanium road bikes quite unlikely. Nevertheless, I often got ego boosts from supportive riders passing by, though my favorite was beating some of those same riders up the hills, fueled by my determination and growing calf muscles.

I tried to celebrate my own personal goals and accomplishments rather than mark myself against others. I was "riding my ride"—arriving safely, averaging above 15 mph, attacking the hills standing up, and finishing strong. I was never to be first, but I was never last either, so why worry? I was out there for me, not for others. These morals and epithets were critical lessons for me, not just in preparing for the physical challenge ahead, but for my more confident new lifestyle. I returned to journaling during this biking phase, another opportunity to reflect on my personal growth and capture my proud moments.

In April 2012, after many months of training, the MS 150 ride was finally here. With nervous excitement I arrived at the starting line, ready to join over 13,000 riders for the most acclaimed bike ride in Texas. I stepped off to the side to collect my thoughts. I focused on all the training I'd done. I was certain I could complete this monumental challenge. The gun blast sliced through the morning nerves and we were off. As the journey began, all solitude was lost and the crowded field constantly surrounded me. This raised the camaraderie and energy level of the event, but also the danger of bumps and accidents. Riders were hailed by roadside cheerleaders, some playing violins, many holding signs of encouragement, others dancing to music blaring Queen's "Fat Bottom Girls" from a bar, while others dressed in flamboyant Mardi Gras-like costumes. Most riders sported lightweight road bikes, a few had heavy hybrids like mine, and some took on the course riding recumbents, along with a unicycle or two dotting the course. Eight and a half hours after the dawn start, I completed the 101-mile first day.

April 21, 2012

Today was AWESOME, the culmination of 12 months of hard work, training, fitness, weight loss, and mental preparation. The wind was definitely a challenge. I heard 20 mph with gusts to 30-plus. I just kept pedaling. I felt really good. Aches and pains for sure. But I rode through each and they seemed to go away. I'm walking tall tonight!

That night, resting on a cot with a hundred others in the Shell tent at the Fayette County Fairgrounds, I couldn't sleep much. It wasn't the noise, but more my normal post-ride fidgetiness, plus a few areas of tenderness and nervous anticipation about the next day's push to Austin. Finally, I got up at 4:30 in the morning, got myself ready, packed up my gear, grabbed some breakfast, and was in line with my bike around 5:30. I was probably one of the first thousand lined up to wait with nervous jitters until they opened the course at 7 AM. Finally on the road, my butterflies subsided, the cold 50-degree night faded, and I hit my stride for the whole day. Once again, I captured my excitement at the end of the day:

April 22, 2012

I've literally been daydreaming about the final stretch to the Capitol for months. Finally, it was here! I took the rolling hills into Austin with vigor. As we crossed under I-35, the final few blocks lay ahead. Next thing I knew, I turned the corner and there it was: the finish line two blocks down, cheering crowds everywhere. I was beaming with excitement and pride. The guy next to me shrieked with joy and that popped the cork on my inhibitions. I screamed and threw my arms up in excitement for the moment and everything it stood for. I high-fived a few onlookers in the crowd as I passed the finish and then, suddenly, it was over. But the fulfillment is still with me. I rode safe, smart, and hard. I held nothing back. I didn't back down from any challenge. I would have done nothing differently. I rode the ride my way, on my "Steel Horse," pumping hard and standing tall, managing my time to my plan, and relishing in the final stretch I had dreamed about for months. What a rush!

As I rode back to Houston in the comfort of our minivan, I thanked my family for their support and especially Jennifer for her encouragement and patience during the many weekends away. Without their support of such an outlandish undertaking and its time commitment, I could never have completed one of my life's greatest accomplishments.

After the MS 150 success, my addictive nature pushed me harder. I continued to ride through the hot summer and then in the two-day Shell-sponsored Bike Around the Bay from east Houston to Galveston and back in October. Bike Around the Bay was a smaller event of about 3,000 riders. The 190-mile ride featured strong headwinds and long boring stretches, countered by the exciting challenge of a half-dozen tall bridges scattered along the otherwise flat route. My focus on hill training certainly paid off, and I notched another major accomplishment on my shrinking belt.

A couple of weeks later I checked in with Shell's fitness staff for an annual wellness exam. At 190 pounds, my weight may have been above some targets, but my muscle tone had reduced my body fat measurements and resulted in their declaration of "optimal." OPTIMAL!

I have never been optimal. I was chubby in utero. I wore husky pants as a pre-teen. I was obese to even morbidly obese my entire adult life. And now, I was "optimal"! I pondered the word as it affixed to my brain. Optimal. What an amazing concept.

"Optimal: Op-ti-mal
Adjective \'ap-te-mel\

Definition of OPTIMAL: most desirable or satisfactory

SYNONYMS: Ace, best, choice, excellent, flawless, greatest, highest, ideal, magnificent, majestic, marvelous, maximum, peak, peerless, perfect, resplendent, select, solid gold, standout, stunning, superior, superlative, top, unrivaled, very best, world class."

I'd never used any of those words when describing myself. In November of 2012, I was told I was "optimal"!

A few months later, I was one of four US employees featured in the "Be Well at Shell" brochure, which celebrated staff using Shell facilities and programs to improve their fitness.

I felt great. I received many compliments, started donating many of my XL clothes, and rebuilt my wardrobe. Though my compulsive nature always had me searching for more, I was now building a new life, replacing my destructive drinking and eating habits of my past. I continued to bike during the winter and added a bit of running as well. Though I missed the next MS 150 in April 2013, due to my niece's Bat Mitzvah in Florida, I made plans to ride the Hotter 'N Hell Hundred in Wichita Falls, Texas. This was going to be brutal. One hundred miles in one day in the grueling 100-degree heat of North Texas. This was not for the faint of heart. After that, I planned another Bike Around the Bay in October with thoughts of a weeklong Red Cross-sponsored ride to New Orleans to follow. The word "moderation" was never really in my vocabulary, but I was "optimal" and happy, so I continued. Until that fateful day in May.

SECTION FIVE – VULNERABLE

CHAPTER 22: COMPLICATED

On May 25, 2013, the Saturday before Memorial Day, I neared the last five miles of my 50-mile bike ride in the nearby countryside. I turned a corner and was greeted by three angry dogs in the middle of the road. Accustomed to outrunning dogs that catch my scent as I bike by their yards, I dismissed the thought of turning around to find an alternate route. But this situation was different. I had no head start or element of surprise. However, machismo kicked in and I sped up to go past the pack. As I got closer, I could see the salivating teeth of the rallying dogs. As they ran barking toward me, I swerved to miss them. However, abrupt turns on a bike at 18 mph don't really mix. I catapulted slow motion over my handlebars and landed on my shoulder. After a few seconds, I instinctively pushed myself up, releasing streams of pain down my arm. I stumbled in circles like a boxer trying to recover from a punch to the head. Once I managed to straighten up, I glanced at the once vicious dogs. Now equally shocked, they had retreated to the other side of the road. I surveyed my bike, hoping to finish my ride. However, as the adrenalin receded and I assessed my situation, I slumped by the side of the rode and called Jennifer for help.

I recapped in an email to my parents and sisters the next day:

May 26, 2013

I tried to pass a pack of dogs on my bike ride in the country yesterday, but the laws of physics did, however, dictate an unplanned dismount and I now have the bruises to prove it: swollen left thigh, scraped up right knee and elbow, and a simple broken left humerus bone (upper arm where it connects to the shoulder). After a day, I can find nothing humorous in this bone break. I went to a small ER near the crash site and after some X-Rays the prognosis is good. No surgery, 6-8 weeks in a sling, and a serious impact on my running and biking schedule. But it certainly could have been worse. No head injury, the dogs didn't see me as easy pickin's and gnaw on my bones, and it could have been my writing arm. Jennifer and the kids are taking great care of me, and keeping me heavily sedated, both of which are helping a lot. Just wanted to "break" the news to you. Otherwise, all is fine!

Sitting at home drifting off to pain reliever-induced sedation, I wondered if this was destiny. I'd skated by so many dogs during my two years of bike riding, not to mention the attack by my girlfriend's Great Dane in third grade. I recalled an article I'd read in my early days of biking. One of the items that stood out was a statement that bike accidents are an inevitable occurrence for those who cycle regularly. The article made sure to note these range from falling off your bike while merely waiting at a stop light to getting your tire stuck in a road groove or the extreme collisions with other bikes or, worse yet, cars. The magazine highlighted that people die every month from bike accidents, while many more get discouraged or sidelined by more modest falls, and everyone gets embarrassed by the simplest of scrapes. Back in 2011, I clipped my bike cleats into a stationary bike in the gym, ready to log some miles, when I lost my balance and tumbled off the bike onto the floor with my left leg still clipped in. No one chuckled more than I did, relieved I had gotten my inevitable bike accident out of the way. Unfortunately, I would not get off so easily.

A few days later after the Memorial Day holiday, I visited several orthopedic specialists who discounted the emergency room diagnosis. I shared an update in another family e-mail:

May 30, 2013

What a week! I can't tell you how many doctors I've seen, how many times people have asked me to stretch out my otherwise immobile arm for X-Rays and ultrasounds (and how quickly I can move from polite to forceful in my reaction). My newfound orthopedist reinterpreted the ER X-Rays and pronounced my upper left arm was broken in three places, my shoulder was dislocated, and the connection into my shoulder was a "big mess." And I'd never even broken a finger up 'til this point.

My surgeon described my injury in graphic detail. Basically, the ball joint at the top of my left arm got "ripped out of the socket, turned 90 degrees, and split open." Ewww! I had the heebie-jeebies all day. So, they could try to reassemble it with plates and screws, but it would require a lot of movement of my veins during surgery just to get to the cracked bones. At this point, my hematologist who monitored my genetic predispositions for blood clotting and hemochromatosis joined the party to reveal that the ultrasound identified a blood clot in my shoulder.

I had been headed toward surgery the following Wednesday, 11 days after the accident, but this was now on hold. I was propelled into an intensive schedule of blood thinners by pill and injections into my midsection to dissolve the clot before surgery. In the meantime, the bits and pieces of my contorted shoulder and arm lay in a sling, sensitive to the slightest movement. Doctors prescribed heavy doses of Vicodin and later two other painkillers to help me manage the throbbing pain during this waiting period.

My thoughts swirled, darting from the pain of my pulsing shoulder to anger at the dogs, and then disappointment at myself for not just turning around. I was apprehensive about the apparent long path ahead. I was fearful that full use of my shoulder and arm might never return. Then I was jolted back to the present by the sharp pain as I tried to readjust my shoulder. Finally, my thoughts landed on determination—to overcome the pain, the fear, and the immobility.

In the meantime, my doctors huddled to plan the surgery. A titanium ball would replace the ball joint at the top of my arm with a rod extending down my arm. The shattered pieces of bone would then be positioned over the rod like pieces of a jigsaw puzzle. With patience and extensive physical therapy, the bone should reconnect around the rod and full range mobility would be possible, though they provided only a 50/50 likelihood of complete success. My doctor deemed my condition "complicated." I liked "optimal" a lot better.

It took two more weeks before the clot was gone and surgery could be scheduled. Such an agonizing period. I couldn't work, I couldn't sleep, and I was drugged up for the pain so I really couldn't function at all. I could only wait for the green light. As I shared with my surgeon when he briefed me in pre-op, I was probably the most eager patient he'd ever had, elated to finally be on the road to recovery that morning of June 20.

Following surgery, I enjoyed a much-needed drug-induced full night of sleep for the first time in three weeks. I woke to a concerned team of doctors.

Surgery seemed to go well, but as a result of the operation, another blood clot had blown my left hand up like a latex glove balloon. The doctors' concern about the clot moving was palpable. My discomfort was intense. I was placed on another round of Lovenox belly shots to dissolve the clot and sent home the next day with instructions to go to the ER if my condition worsened. My arm was in a bulky, nearly immovable black Velcro sling that ironically looked like the padding someone would wear when training police dogs to lunge at escaping criminals.

Meanwhile my sleep-deprived body dozed off only from sheer exhaustion. I could not manage to lie down, so my naps were in our den recliner surrounded by many strategically placed pillows. My mind sluggishly shifted between shoulder pain, arm discomfort, and a preoccupation with worst-case scenarios regarding the clot in my hand. Granted, I had my share of unexpected twists and turns through the ordeal. Nevertheless, I fretted over possible new clots, arthritis, and nerve damage in my persistently aching left hand, and another impending shoulder surgery given my doctor's 10-year warranty. This became as much a mental recovery as a physical one.

I could only think of myself and my own struggles. Thankfully, Noah and Gwen were at summer camps. Madolyn flew off to visit prospective college campuses with a cousin, a trip I was looking forward to leading but had to arrange others to host instead. This quieted the house while Jennifer and her Aunt Marilyn nursed my every need. However, I could tell I was causing great distress amongst them. I sensed their huddling in the kitchen and upstairs, worrying, crying, and consoling each other. This was my routine for many days as the medically induced haze kept me from any real activity.

I don't generally consider myself a spiritual person. Perhaps because of this, I don't really remember my dreams. I typically go to sleep, toss and turn, and wake up. Period. But one late June night was different. Jennifer noticed an awe-inspiring bright purple sky and lured Aunt Marilyn out to look at it. Shortly thereafter, I drifted away for a two-hour respite, during which I had an especially vivid dream in which the swelling in my left hand disappeared. Granted, my preoccupation with the inflammation since surgery made this a frequent topic at the time, but as I woke, I stared down at my hand and the swelling had indeed gone down considerably. Within a couple of days, it was gone completely. The risk had passed. Now I could re-focus on healing my arm and shoulder.

A week later, the pain in my shoulder had finally dissipated to localized discomfort. After a month on three different painkillers I was increasingly frustrated by the medicated fog I found myself in. I announced to Jennifer it was time to drop the meds and return to a more conscious state. That first day off meds was delightful. I was able to function, understand, and communicate like normal. However, by the next day, I was not feeling so well. It wasn't really pain. I just became weak and lethargic and then alternated between hot and cold spells. By the third day, I was sweating profusely, stripping clothes to my underwear and then an hour later I was shaking with chills and wrapping up in several blankets. I became weaker and eventually struggled to make it just 10 yards to the bathroom. How could this be? I had just been biking over 100 miles. I was in the best shape of my life. Did I have a new clot that was traveling? Was my body shutting down? Was I dying? Something was very wrong! I was scared and I could see from Jennifer's face she was freaking out too.

A morning visit to the ER and then to my hematologist finally confirmed a suspicion: I was in withdrawal—opioid withdrawal! Oh my god, I didn't even realize all these pills were opioids. I'd fallen prey to a national epidemic without knowing. Maybe I was just too drugged up to understand, but my weeks of heavy drug use were not to be taken lightly. The immediate termination of these drugs had thrown my body into shock. I had failed to share my compulsive history with the doctors, which may have contributed to this particular addiction and shocking withdrawal. I had certainly not coordinated my cold turkey approach with them either. The doctors provided the option for me to return to the meds and follow a prescribed weaning protocol or, alternatively I could persist through another few days of withdrawals until my body fully recovered. With the comfort of knowing what was going on, I decided to push through.

I continued to strip and bundle up in rapid succession. Finally, the shakes and sweats broke, and I resumed my recovery. What a bummer, all those drugs to the point of withdrawals and no enjoyment of the high that should have come along with it. But I was lucky to be able to extract myself from what could have spiraled down into an uncontrollable obsession. As with my college gambling and when I turned down the bongs being passed around at my sister's house when in high school, I seem to have an inner voice that has kept me from catastrophe.

A couple of days later, still exhausted from my drug recovery and extremely uncomfortable as I struggled with the bulky sling resting across my mid-section day and night, Jennifer and I finally ventured out to the doctor for a checkup. My orthopedist's nurse ushered me to the X-Ray room, which I was to learn was code for modern torture session. After removing my padded sling for the first time since surgery, I was instructed to hold my arm up with my other hand while two X-Rays were taken. So far, so good. Then the fun began: spreading my arm out like a chicken wing so they could X-Ray the joint. Not fun. I did call the tech a bitch, but she pretended not to hear, knowing she would take her revenge on the tabletop X-Rays to come.

Once I managed to get down on the table, I had to straighten my arm and then shift it out about 60 degrees from my body. "Let's put a towel roll under your arm and I will just slide it out one centimeter," she said. When she did that without much wincing on my part she asked about another centimeter, then another.

"I know exactly what you're up to," I declared.

She kept this tactic up until I flinched from the pain, clenching my fist and teeth. "I sure hope you took your pain meds before coming here!" she suggested. After I chuckled to myself, she continued to contort me in all sorts of ways until her job was complete. "All done! Hop up and make your way to the doctor's office."

Ha! I don't generally hop. It took gradual movement to get up these days. I was sweating from the workout as I returned my arm into its casing.

Jennifer joined me on the way to the doctor's office. "How were the X-Rays, Steve?"

"Because I love you, I'll say it was fine. But, because I'm striving to be more open and transparent, I'll admit it made the bike accident feel like a walk in the park."

"Sorry," she said.

As we continued to walk toward the doctor's room Jennifer slowed, turned to look at me, sniffing, and exclaimed, "You stink!"

"You know, I noticed a stench in the X-Ray room. I realized it must be me. It was the first time in a month that I've actually opened my left armpit!"

"Well, I think something died up there," she offered.

As we entered my orthopedist's office, I could only nod my head.

My doctor reveled at my shrunken left hand and marveled at my successful detox. Reviewing my X-Rays, he indicated my bones seemed to be healing in all the right places. A good checkup on my road to rehab. Relieved that perhaps the worst was over, I reflected on the likely impact of my new appliance:

10. I may be accused of cheating with an extra turn in skee-ball.

9. I'll become a transformer (not in a good way) if I get an MRI.

8. You bring the six-pronged metal playing pieces and we'll play ball and jacks.

7. It'll be me slowing you down at airport security.

6. I'll need to drink a shot of WD-40 every week.

5. In very cold weather, frost may appear on my left shoulder.

4. My new look will include magnets down my left arm.

3. I'm now only 98% "Made in America."

2. My Titanium is a natural hedge against the slumping US dollar.

1. "I am Titanium" is a lot catchier than "I am Osseous Tissue and Marrow."

Within a couple of weeks, it was time to start physical therapy. I was eager to see what PT would involve and excited to move to the next phase of my recovery toward normalcy.

CHAPTER 23: PLACEBO

After an hour of introductions and measurements, the "yank and crank" sessions began with my dominatrix therapist, Jovita. She was a strong, slender, Indian lady with a pleasant but most determined disposition.

I captured an early session in my journal:

July 09, 2013

Therapy starts with a 10-minute hot towel wrap, which sounds soothing except the towel is so thick it feels like my shoulder is lying on a rock—a hot molten lava rock. She then gently picks up my left arm and shakes it in waves, which is strangely soothing. If only it would last. Next, she grabs my arm and bends it at the elbow, and I know the real fun has just begun. After five minutes lying flat on my back on the bench, she moves the arm over the shoulder. I usually like this because it feels like I'm making progress when my arm disappears out of sight. Instead, it's the warm feeling which disappears as she continues to push my arm further. She pushes to the point of a grimace (mine) and a chuckle (hers), stops, reverses, and then comes back for just a smidgen more. At this point she usually either remarks it feels quite loose today and this is the farthest it's moved or says it's quite tight. The recognition makes me proud and hopeful; the scolding makes me wonder if progress is ending short of full recovery.

When I roll back over, we are usually on the homestretch. She tries to rip a bit more scar tissue, and then says she's done torturing me. I do a few of my prescribed home exercises. She shows me a new one, and then we call it a day. She moves on to a couple of her other dozen victims of the day and I move on to recuperate my body through Tylenol, stretches, heating pads, and scorching hot showers which seem to temporarily melt the rigid metal inside of me.

I'm going to log three of these torture sessions per week for at least the next couple of months. I'm (literally) torn during these sessions. They are painful, sometimes to the point of tears—not crying, but just tears that seep out the corner of my eyes. It's scary, too, as I don't know how far Jovita will push me each day, but it's exciting to make progress on my much-anticipated road to recovery. My obsessive nature is all-in on this venture!

At home, my exercises included pendulum swings, arm and wrist bends to keep my hand relaxed, and then some big ball rolls (rolling a large aerobic ball out and back 60 times). Finally, I head to the bedroom for Mary Poppins (pushing my left arm back as far as possible with the pointy end of an umbrella digging into my hand) and the Floppy Fish (where I lie on the bed on my belly and squeeze my shoulder blades together as I raise my head). Given the lack of muscles in my left arm, I'm merely lying there with my face planted in my pillow. As tempting as it was to dose off, my unending stiffness ensured that wouldn't happen. As instructed, I did these exercises for about 20 minutes six times a day, though I usually did them more often just to relieve the tension in my shoulder that built up throughout the day.

After another successful doctor's check-up a couple of weeks later, Jovita moved from passive to aggressive therapy aimed at rebuilding muscles and regaining independence. I was now wearing my sling only half the day and hoped to be fully weaned off by the following week. So Jovita declared: "I'll be stepping up the cranking," clearly fully implementing the term aggressive. I felt like the Tasmanian Devil—arms going in every direction throughout my session. Finally, it was time for some self-inflicted pain. She introduced some new home exercises to build strength, including using a pulley to raise my hand, and crawling my fingers up a wall. My 20 minutes of home exercise now stretched toward 30 minutes every three hours and the house was beginning to look like a cheap gym, with pulleys, aerobic balls, umbrellas, and towels strewn throughout.

Though the pain slowly receded, even part time work was still a couple of weeks off. I tried to distract myself from my preoccupation with recovery by journaling and blogging my updates and adventures to family and friends. It was the most writing I'd done since the train commutes in London and rekindled my interest in serious writing which had been dormant since my high school days at the school newspaper.

Meanwhile, during these two months since the accident, I'd tried everything to get a good night's sleep—over the counter meds, meditation, and pillows of every shape and size. I tested all the different bedding in the house, including recliners and even our outdoor chaise lounge, but unlike Goldilocks, I could neither find one that was just right, nor even close. The many pieces of my reassembled shoulder and arm could not achieve states of harmony to enable long lasting sleep. Inevitably, within several minutes discomfort or stiffness set in. If I was fortunate to doze off for an hour, my arm felt like a rusty crank that hadn't been turned in years when I woke. After six weeks of this, I was desperate for sleep and returned to the doctor for help.

After reminding her of my recent opioid addiction, I was prescribed Ambien with the forewarning to take only as directed. She ensured me I was destined to get many consecutive hours of sleep. Though I'd never taken Ambien before, I'd seen it in action as one of my co-workers used to pop an Ambien at the beginning of long transatlantic flights. She was out for a solid six hours. The pharmacist agreed this should do the trick: "Give it 30 to 60 minutes and you should get six to 10 hours of uninterrupted sleep. As a matter of fact, you should be careful as people have been known to sleepwalk from such a deep sleep." Fantastic!

So that night, Jennifer barricaded the bedroom door with our ottoman as I took my first pill, expecting Ambien would finally do the trick. After giddily preparing the bed, wishing my wife a good night and that I'd see her in the morning, I eventually drifted off… only to wake just an hour later. After another failed attempt, I now believed Ambien was French for "placebo!" I dismissed my inclination to double the dose and resumed my life of haphazard napping.

As my rehabilitation proceeded in search of productive normalcy, I began my return to work in three-hour increments. These short stints served as a morale booster, given how far I'd come since surgery two months earlier. Anxious to tackle some work, I was however unable to accomplish any tasks those first couple of weeks. I was often exhausted, both from the commute with a friend, as well as from searching for places to do my exercises to avoid the stiffening pain of rigor mortis. Still unable to sleep, we decided to schedule some day trips after work to tire me out completely.

Welcome to the unique world of Vera Bradley, that wonderful apparel and accessory store. We happened to visit during their grand opening weekend. How lucky!

As we moved through the store, we viewed the impressive wall units of products. Who knew there could be so many purses? I realized they had each style for every size, which increased by one square inch increments from tiny, Barbie size, to gargantuan. Then they multiplied that by applying a half dozen colors and patterns to each style via some kind of random pattern generator. I'd discovered there were rules to mixing and matching such patterns. Do it right and you were en vogue; wrong and you were just plain tacky. I suggest a Garanimal-style matching system to save customers from embarrassment at the least, and social stoning at the extreme.

I followed Jennifer to the back of the store before I realized I was in the middle of a feeding frenzy. Dozens of women were tearing through purses, backpacks, luggage, and even waterproof gardening bags (if it's raining, don't garden!) and gloves (really, one must wear Vera Bradley gloves to get dirty beyond recognition?). To save myself, I backed up about 10 feet, finding myself in line with a few other jaw-dropped men. The guy next to me noticed my sling and asked what happened. "Vera Bradley opening day yesterday!" I responded. He just nodded.

Granted, this much-needed addition to the Houston Premium Outlet Mall offered 40% off most items that weekend, but some things were still a bit ridiculous. Topping that list were the two-dozen Vera Bradley pencils for $18! What happened to some good ol' yellow No. 2s for a buck? But how tacky would that be!

Having survived the Vera Bradley field trip, the next week we pressed our luck with an afternoon at IKEA. I joined Jennifer and Gwen for a quick shopping spree to pick up a few things. However, there's nothing quick about IKEA and it's really not a place to go on the spur of the moment. In advance, I suggest wearing comfortable shoes, going to the bathroom upon arrival, and bringing a canteen and do-it-yourself colostomy bag, just in case.

(Un)fortunately, we found what we were seeking around the first few bends. So, now we were forced to obey the "one way" signs and continue down the yellow brick road. Surprisingly, especially for a furniture store, I just couldn't find a chair where I could rest. I suspected I'd have to assemble one with Swedish instructions. Instead I opted to race ahead, hoping to trade in an extended stroll down the dizzying path for some rest at the end.

I realized the "to exit" signs were just to transfer into different time zones, not actually to leave the store. Eventually near the finish line, with ABBA's *Mamma Mia* songs running through my brainwashed head, I passed the Swedish grocery. Visions of the Muppets' Swedish chef danced in my head.

Having survived the maze, I got my rewarding piece of cheese (a delicious soft pretzel), after which I found a corner and completed some much-needed stretches. Then I waited for Jennifer and Gwen, who were not so fortunate in navigating the maze. They had to make a dash for a bathroom, after which they had to search for their cart, only to find it had been emptied and restocked in their absence. Argh, those damn efficient Swedes!

Unfortunately, even this extended trip on top of a half day of work did not induce sleep. I was craving sleep like I used to crave chocolate or a vodka tonic.

Recovery from the bike accident, surgery, opioid withdrawal, and sleep deprivation proved to be a long and arduous path. I wished these were the only new challenges I had to tackle.

CHAPTER 24: FEAR

Oh, to be invincible. To take on life with a sense of immortality—no particular concern for the aches and pains of aging or fear of death. When did that change for me?

It seemed like yesterday when I was eight and Roger and I set up ramps and jumped wagons with our bikes. Or when I happily took up my sisters' challenge to bike ride head-on into a spruce bush. Or when I was 11 and conducted a science experiment: could a 100-pound 11-year-old drink an 8-ounce glass of bourbon? Or when I was in college drinking pure grain hunch punch after donating a pint of blood.

Then, suddenly, confronted by three dogs, I decided not to turn around. In that moment, my invincibility vanished. My bike accident and recovery underscored the fragility of my health like never before. The deviations like blood clots, opioid withdrawals, and sleep deprivation aged me both physically and mentally. During my recovery, I was not only battling the challenges to repair my shoulder, but I was confronting new fears of growing older and losing my physical capabilities or mental edge. The fear of recurring and more complicated illnesses rattled me. Beyond that, I could not rid myself of the fear of being preoccupied, of constantly worrying if this ache or pain might be the beginning of a downward slope that would not correct itself. What scared me most was not death itself, though I was assuredly not ready to leave my family and dreams behind. It was the fear of fear.

Until my bike accident I had not even broken a finger. Now, I was struggling primarily with the mental challenges of the whole ordeal. Would I be physically restored to my previous capabilities? Or was this the beginning of my decline? I always considered myself pretty tough. I believed I could handle life's rough spots if they were thrust upon me. However, what I discovered was that I was not as tough as I thought. I was a stubborn male who could hold my emotions inside to avoid burdening others with my worries, but that was not toughness. I cowered at needles and blood. I worried constantly about each twinge and hurt. Yet this was only my first life-battle with true pain and, to some extent, mortality. If I were fortunate enough to live to a ripe old age, what would that look like? Would I crumble under the pressure? Under the enormous weight of inevitable decline, loss of function, and approaching death?

I tried to work through this on my own but found I was only spiraling further downward. I knew from London that mental stress could show itself in many physical ways. This surely contributed to my excruciating struggle to get a good night's sleep throughout the summer of 2013.

In late summer, I decided that I would seek some outside guidance. A therapist I saw tried to comfort me by saying "this too shall pass," and that the whole experience would be a valuable story to lean upon when future illnesses and hardships of old age come to bear. Building my toolbox for more serious ailments in the future was certainly not very comforting. She suggested I lean on intuition and spirituality to be confident in my recovery. However, my intuition had always been poor. While Jennifer maintained great respect for her instincts and spiritual signs which she observed, my intuition was more akin to a Houston worm who was immensely confident that crossing an asphalt road in 100-degree August heat was a good idea. At least I was aware of my poor instincts and tended to use premonitions as cautions rather than gospel. Hence, I continued to be preoccupied with aging, but without paying $150 an hour.

Though I went through periods of obligatory faith as a kid and teen, I never considered myself spiritual as an adult. Perhaps trained by years of corporate structure, I was driven by facts and data more so than heart and soul. I relied more on my logic, my conscience, my core belief systems and ethos. I wanted to believe. I thought there must be comfort in that. Perhaps if I had faith, I would have had more courage to take chances and I would have endured less stress to wear me down. I did respect those who believed, assuming they weren't proselytizing to unwelcoming masses—including myself. Sometimes it saddened me, this lack of faith, and yet I also couldn't fake this sentiment and connection.

Nevertheless, during this arduous recovery at the height of my despair and trough of my depression, I ventured out to our synagogue's weekday morning services. It was interesting that, just as I had returned to synagogue in 1990 to seek some support after my second DUI, I was once again coming back for guidance. Perhaps there was a glimmer of belief in me, or maybe it was just a sign of desperation. I wasn't sure if I was going to pray or to seek assistance, camaraderie, direction, or just a reflective atmosphere, but it felt like the right place to be.

As a first timer to the morning minyan service, I was greeted and treated very nicely. I was encircled by men and women in their 70s to 90s, most sporting various apparatuses: walkers, hearing aids, wrist guards, and special boots for circulation. So I felt at home with my padded sling, though I presumed the health of many of them was on a slow, downward trajectory while I counted on mine being temporary. Still, we could have put on a medical supply fashion show.

How did they get to this point? How do we all get to that point? How do we deal with our loss of invincibility? How about the frustration and despair that even I—a generally healthy, though complicated specimen—had been wrestling with lately? Do they deal with that daily or get numb to it? Is my current ordeal part of that numbing process?

I was trying not to compare myself to an 80-year-old, but I thought my bike accident and morning minyan visit both provided a peek forward. It was a bit chilling. Couldn't I just be invincible for another few decades? I left the service with little guidance and more questions than answers.

Still struggling, I opted to return the following week seeking solitude and peace. That day the service began with the Book of Deuteronomy which covered the Hebrews wandering around the desert for 40 years along with God passing down many new laws through Moses. It talked about Moses stating his belief in his plan to find and conquer Canaan, though later he admitted that the plan was faulty. In the end it really was God's will, both as a form of punishment and as a fresh start in the new land, that none of the original group ever saw Canaan.

I finally accepted a few helpful tidbits:

1. **Be patient.** It may seem like 40 years, sometimes, but my mobility and routine will return far sooner than that, and I have the luxury of air conditioning and leavened bread.

2. **Be resilient.** Moses recognized his errors and "manned up" to them. It made him a truly great leader. It was amazing that he maintained a relatively strong following during such turbulent times, despite a few squabbles and a Golden Calf here and there, in order to lead his people to the future State of Israel. If Moses could believe and maintain that kind of faith for 40 years, surely I could do the same to see my promised land of milk and honey—or at least mobility and sleep.

3. **Be faithful**. God, or Nature if you will, continues to pass down and maintain many laws. We all must adhere to these laws. For me, at this moment, these were laws of healing. There was no miracle or overnight cure, but if I worked hard and was patient the healing would come. Stop worrying, have a bit of faith in something—even myself—and release those things which I can't control. Use my energy on things I can control—attitude and therapy with vigor—and I will have my own fresh start soon enough.

I do love this historical and philosophical stuff, especially after traveling the land and seeing some of the sites during our two trips to Israel. My morning minyan visit gave me a chance to reconnect with Judaism and contemplate my religious beliefs. While I don't believe in God himself, I do relate to Judaism's rich history and many traditions. Thus, I still consider myself an active Jew. As a history buff, I connect with the past of the Jewish people who like many others thousands of years ago believed in a higher power that helped explain the unexplainable in a pre-science age and gave hope and direction to an otherwise simple and rudderless world. As a people, they bonded and developed holidays, traditions, and ethos around their belief. For this culture they were often persecuted, an act each religion or tribe likely conveyed upon the other. Under the weight of this persecution, many religions folded into others or faded into history entirely.

Judaism was left as a resilient but relatively small sect of people even up to modern times. Escaping persecution, Jews migrated first from the Holy Land to Babylon and then clockwise around the Mediterranean Sea as they were stripped of rights, enslaved, beaten and killed, until they had exhausted the circle in eastern Europe including Poland,

Ukraine, Lithuania, and Russia. Jews finally started to migrate back to the Levant and over to North America as a response to the 19th century pogroms. Those remaining were subject to Hitler's Holocaust. Survivors championed the creation of the state of Israel, and battle anti-Semitism around the world to this day. I am a believer in the history that was so well rooted in their belief in God centuries and millennia ago. What courageous people. What an inspiring story.

CHAPTER 25: DEATH

As August wore on, my mobility was improving. I relied on my patience, resilience, and faith in the process to continue my vigorous physical therapy to capture that last twenty percent. In the midst of this climb, Mom and Dad helped guide me through the worst of my rehabilitation. We talked frequently. Sometimes we compared our ailments and laughed. Best of all, I just knew they were there for me.

But on the last day of August, I received a call from my sister Gayle that was shattering. Dad had succumbed to an infection at nearly 85 and, without any notice, died in hospital. I hadn't seen him since the previous Thanksgiving, due to my focus on work and bike riding. Though he was certainly aging, my last vision of Dad was of a frail man, yet with plenty more mileage on his mind and body and lots more to share with his family. I never considered Dad my constant or my rock growing up, but as my personal journey to know and love myself took hold since returning from London, I realized how truly alike we were. Unbeknownst to him, he had become my role model for the person I had struggled to be. Now, he was gone.

I had grown comfortable being alone with my thoughts and reflections, but suddenly a sense of loneliness overtook me. I now understood the difference between the two terms—alone and loneliness. I felt like I had so much to say and ask my dad. I wished I'd said "thank you" for the principles he provided me. Though I'd wavered quite a bit in my life, those values saw me through very dark periods. But now he was gone.

My dad, while not flashy or boisterous, was my hero because he had such personal pride. He seemed simple; he did not even have a middle name. But he was honest and loyal to his core. He always did everything he could to provide a middle-class lifestyle to Mom and us four kids. Much of this happened during some challenging family times in the late '70s. He did jobs he didn't enjoy and worked hours he loathed to ensure our standard of living. Yet he did it without objection. If that's stubborn, I was all in.

I visited Birmingham a few months after his passing, searching for answers. I went to Oak Mountain State Park, where Dad had dragged me out many summer days gone by, to write a letter:

November 28, 2013

Dearest Dad,

Today, I've come to visit you at Peavine Falls. It's a beautiful clear, chilly day at Oak Mountain. I piloted the hike down to the falls with the experience and familiarity that will never leave me. I remember the narrowing path, each of the twists and turns, the trees I held as I navigated around exposed roots. I hear the birds chirping in the distance. I see the tree branches filled with an array of colors, waving in the occasional breeze. The trickle of the falls below signaling the dryness of the summer as it fades away.

I hear you questioning why I came so ill prepared. Where is my water? My map? My compass and snack bag? I chuckle, and yet, I am here, with you. Perhaps one last time.

It's been five years since I've been here. I feel close to you here. I miss you terribly, each and every day. I think of you and your unflinching love. I think of your resilient, devoted personality that you passed on to me. I didn't recognize the gift back then and, if I did, I didn't want it. But I carry you with me every day, proudly. I stare into the trees as I contemplate my letter to you. They seem to be leaning toward me, as if they embody you and you are striving to listen to my unspoken words. I think you would be proud of the work I've done over the past few years to fix my life. I've tried to listen to what you taught me, your subtle yet powerful examples. I look down into my laptop screen, and the reflection is my own, yet I see you— your thick brows, prominent nose, and smile which you can't help but twist until I laugh.

It's funny, as a kid I felt like perhaps we spent too much time together—dragged off on hikes on dirty, bumpy trails without TV or friends. Our times were spent with agonizing silence. Yet now I realize that in between your long work weeks, you chose to spend time with me. Time away from the rat race of life and the stress of a house full of teenagers and real world issues and come to nature with me. Nature provided the peace and tranquility you yearned for; the peace I'm now realizing I, too, crave. To instill appreciation of the brilliance of nature in me for the rest of my life was indeed a gift. Ours was perhaps an unspoken love in many ways. We rarely talked in depth about girls, life, money, dreams, concerns, aches, or pains. Yet, now, I feel like we understand each other. That our thoughts, cares, hurts and coping passed between us to some degree, albeit with a heart wrenching three-decade lag.

I've struggled to recuperate from my bike accident, yet I struggle even more to reconcile your passing. But sitting here, with you, I know now what I need to do. As you did with your life, I need to continue to dedicate my life to my family—to feel their warmth and to support their dreams. I've also thought a lot about our discussion a few years ago when you shared your life's regret that you never pursued your love of music, to share your talents with the world, to see where that passion might take you. Given the time at home recovering over the last few months, I've begun journaling and writing again. You've inspired me to write a book, to capture my story for my family and myself.

I wish we had talked more, to know more of your past—your childhood, your relations with your parents, your battles and your eventual acceptance of your own personality that I so reluctantly received from you. What drove you, what inspired you, what saddened you, what made you most happy? We didn't talk about this openly, but I suspect I know, as my answers to such questions emerged from yours.

Forever more, I wear your wedding ring on my right hand, a tribute to my unrecognized right-hand man all these years and in hopes of emulating your character and making you proud of me as a husband, father, and mensch.

I'm ready to walk back up the trail now.

I love you lots and carry you with me always.

Talk to you soon!

Love, Stephen

The loss of such a formidable person in my life was especially difficult during my ongoing therapy and my return to work. Dad's passing continued to leave a hole in my life that was compounded by Mom's plummeting health over the next year. She was lonely and fragile. She had many ailments that brought her in and out of the hospital. Michelle paid frequent visits to her assisted living home while all siblings bickered about Mom's future plans and the money to cover them. It was a frustrating period where divisiveness, more so than bonding, took the lead.

However, in late December 2014, I sat in a hospital room watching Mom, immobile, bruised, and wishing to die. She repeated that it is "awful, painful. I don't want to do this anymore," and beseeched Dad, "Richard," and "Oh, God," sometimes in her drowsiness.

"Stephen, I'm so glad you came to visit. I've missed you. But I'm ashamed you are seeing me like this," she mumbled as she looked away.

"Mom, I love you. I want to be here with you. For whatever you need." I reached out for her soft, delicate hand.

She turned back to me, with a tear rolling down her cheek.

I looked at her face and struggled to see my mom, the mother who raised me, cared for me, supported me through my school, my lost sibling bets, my early drinking. And yet she was there to celebrate my success in school and work and family. She, who had always supported me, almost without fail, was dying.

She wanted to hear about the kids but lacked the focus to listen, drawn to her own pain and misery by what ailed her. She lacked the hope to be better, to eat, to move, or to dream of a return to "normalcy," knowing that it would likely be much less than her previous normalcy yet better than her next.

During the hours by her bedside, I journaled a note to Mom:

December 26, 2014 7:55 PM

I think of you and Dad often. I must admit most of the time it's Dad. I think because as a kid, you and I spent so many wonderful times together—talking, playing jacks, going for walks, getting toys at Smith's. It was magical for me. My memories, at least the ones I choose to remember, are pure joy. I guess I just wasn't ready to connect with Dad at that time. I credit you for trying and Dad for giving me the space he knew I needed. Now that I reflect on my life and personality quirks, I see Dad in the mirror every day. If it weren't for your gift of gentle nudging, I likely wouldn't have even spent the time with Dad that I did. I thank you for that.

The screen flashed good blood pressure, good oxygen, and good pulse, yet she was dying. Her kidneys were failing. She was suffering from congestive heart failure. Her heart was under attack. Her will to live was gone. The doctors were trying to get the fluid off her heart in time to save her, but this would be a battle that could only end one way. The question was when, and perhaps how, if it mattered. Maybe not soon, but she who had stood by me and my dad and our family, working and providing, was running out of will—and time.

She just wanted peace and time with Dad. She wanted to say her goodbyes and move on to a better place without pain and the yearning of vibrant family memories gone by. She was sleeping a lot. She was exhausted and needed the rest. And perhaps as the weekend went on and the diuretics worked, she would feel better. But she would awake soon. To pain and discomfort. And she would moan, squirm as if to leave her body, implore God and anyone who would listen, and then fade into a deeper sleep once again.

December 27, 2014 8:15 AM

As the years moved on, I don't think I was there for you like you had always been there for me. You cleaned my scraped knees, picked me off the street after I plunged into a bush on my bike, wiped the vomit off my face after my first drink at 11, and comforted me when I had to recover from my bike accident and surgery. Yet I wasn't there for you to repay all you did for me. Oh, I talked to you on the phone weekly, but we were both physically and emotionally distant. I really couldn't appreciate, not to mention help, with the struggles you were going through.

The top of her face looked like my mom. Smooth forehead, eyes, and glasses through which she had watched me grow. The lower part was squished without her top dentures, looking more like her mom, Grandma Jean, on her deathbed. Her lower lip over her upper, almost touching her nose, as if in a constant frown.

She blew out exhaust from her mouth like a runner, yet she couldn't stand and seemed numb to the fact that her feet were out in front of her, no longer aching to move. It had been weeks since she'd walked. Would her circulation keep up or would she lose limbs to diabetes like her mother?

December 27, 2014 1:10 PM

I'd been so wrapped up in my work, that I struggled to stay connected with Jennifer and the kids, and that meant I just couldn't muster the time, or more likely the courage, to reinsert myself into your lives in a meaningful way. This was especially the case your last year as I felt the weight of middle age stripping me of my invincibility. Listening to your pains only exacerbated my worries. I am sorry I could not rise above my own fears to be there in your many times of need. I think of this often with sadness.

What a horrible way to end a life that was filled with love for her husband and kids. She knew she did her best but surely had regrets, like us all. But she had undying love for everyone.

She loved watching football, Alabama Crimson Tide and Monday Night Football. She loved knitting and antiquing and garaging and had Delft and mirror collections throughout the house. I remembered talking to her from Tuscaloosa to celebrate my job offer from Shell. I remembered playing pennies on our sidewalk waiting for Dad to come home.

December 27, 2014 7:59 PM

I know I cannot change the past. I can only remember, learn from it, and strive to be there for the ones I love and can still touch today. I'm glad I'm here with you today.

She was not deeply philosophical but was troubled for much of her life with agoraphobia and depression. She and Dad made a great team. They struggled together to provide a middle-class lifestyle for a family of six while each of us provided our own adolescent challenges in search of ourselves.

On Sunday, my last day in Birmingham, Mom was feeling better. Her doctors expected a rollercoaster to the end. Perhaps selfishly, I had not shared that with her. She was having a better day. Couldn't she have that? Tomorrow would come. Meanwhile, couldn't we have conversations without talk of death and her wanting to die? We shared, talked about the kids, and watched all the videos, bringing a smile to her delicate face. After she reminded me how I'd been there for her when she was in the hospital before being diagnosed with agoraphobia, I "washed" her hair one last time and said my goodbyes to her teary eyes.

I got to my rental car in the garage and wept. Though the doctors said it could be days or weeks, I knew it was the last time I would see my mom.

After my days on the edge with Mom, I had to return to Houston to handle some work items and prepare for our family trip to Kansas City. My oldest sister Michelle was due back in town and Renee was planning to see Mom the next week.

On my way to the airport, I swung by to say hello to Dad. I put pebbles on his headstone from each of my family, my siblings, and Mom, and I wept. "Dad, I'm trying to make you proud. Miss you. Sorry I wasn't there for you at the end. I'm trying to help Mom. I'm working hard with a positive attitude to help support family like you did. Mom misses you. She will see you soon. I love you." Finally, I scribbled my last note in my journal:

December 28, 2014 12:32 PM

Soon, I trust you will be holding hands with Dad, playing sweet music together, and looking down upon us with a smile and sense of accomplishment, as you should.

A few days after my return, on January 1, 2015, Mom lost her battle with kidney disease and diabetes. It was a jarring loss. With Dad gone 16 months prior, suddenly I felt like a tree leaning horribly, pulled from its roots after a storm. Jennifer grieved as well at her loss of such close in-laws. She helped to prop me up, but she couldn't provide the roots to right me. That would take time.

These losses were overwhelming. I missed them so. I saw their faces in crowds. I yearned to hear their voices. My thoughts of death, of fear, of losing my invincibility forever were consuming me.

I've lived much of my life battling my own demons and now I'm finally making strides to be a more confident and healthy family man. How could I continue doing that and set these fears and losses aside?

When I returned to Houston, Gwen brought home a beautifully painted shiny black box with gold lettering of my initials. I was drawn to this box. It seemed like the perfect home for my paranoias to reside and let me rest. I wrote down my worries and fears—concerns about leaving family behind, dealing with pain and loss of faculties, fears of the unknown and of having regrets. Then I closed the box. There are so many coats of paint on my shiny black box of fears it would appropriately have to be pried open with a knife if I'm ever ready to release the demons within. I placed it on the corner of my bathroom counter as a reminder that I'd set aside all the worries of death so I could get on with life.

CHAPTER 26: HEROES

I hate to live in fear. I feel like I've done that too often in my life. Determined to overcome, I considered my last entry into my black box of fears: Having Regrets. I decided that my greatest areas of remorse focused around my health, my assertiveness, my relationships, and my lack of family time. Each had been a shortcoming of the past which I wanted to better understand and address in my future.

One of my lingering regrets had to do with my health. For years, my work hard/play hard approach deteriorated my body to the brink of disaster. Though I'd made considerable progress since returning to Houston, my bike accident posed a significant setback that I'd had to overcome to keep my health on the right track.

Perhaps just as detrimental was my aversion to conflict or debate, which emanated from a combination of my introversion, my shyness, and my years of growing up without developing skills for conflict resolution. Sure, I would begrudgingly emerge to coach the occasional malcontent at work or offer my opinion when called upon at meetings. But my approach was more as an unwilling participant rather than one prepared to openly contest opinions or even fight for my own positions or ideals. Avoiding conflict had limited my potential and my sense of satisfaction.

Along the way, some of the most significant and nagging misgivings regarded unfulfilled relationships. This certainly included those I had wronged like Roger Bates, my childhood best friend who I abandoned in middle school. Rising above the crowd and standing up for the people that mean the most to me must be non-negotiable. Perhaps that takes courage, especially in eighth grade, but it's a personal principle I can't waver on.

Also, I often pondered those I had vilified for seemingly doing wrong to me, including Kenneth Braman and Nigel Foster. Through these experiences, I've realized we are all human. We have our own style and approach. I don't believe any of them were malicious but made decisions because they thought they were right. Maybe they didn't receive good counsel or involve others in some key decisions, but I myself could be blamed for the same shortcomings by some of my staff in the past. These situations and people caused me a lot of grief and stress, but my inability to let these items go and flow into history only compounded my anxiety over the years.

Most importantly, I continued to lament the time I'd missed with my kids and Jennifer. The anguish I laid upon Jennifer, especially in London, sat in the pit of my stomach always. My family was everything to me. Jennifer, my partner in life, had helped me find my way every time. Now that I'd come through the darkest of times, I often shared my remorse and determination to do better, to be there and truly share our lives together. Jennifer thought I made too much of the grief I conveyed on her, but the looks and questions after my drunk wandering in London and her ultimate rebuke in Prague are burnt in my mind. Perhaps my dad had set such a high bar in always ensuring family was first. Meeting my own expectations, providing love and support for her, and spending quality time with each of the kids were now top priorities.

I realized, perhaps too late, that Dad was one of my heroes, quietly guiding me through life's challenges. Maybe now was a perfect time to enlist more heroes.

Gwen was my hero because she did what she wanted. Not just because she was stubborn, but because she didn't recognize social standards. She said what was on her mind. She loved those who made her feel good and disregarded those who didn't appear to provide positive energy to her.

In 2014 Gwen was 20, thriving at Houston's Down Syndrome Academy. She had blossomed from a shy and stubborn girl to a confident young lady. Now, the girl who was too reserved to walk across a stage at a kid's summer camp was singing Christina Aguilera's "I Am Beautiful" to standing ovations and teary eyes, both in front of 400 attendants at her school's annual Cinderella Ball and on board our summer Caribbean cruise. Gwen's post-high school transition introduced questions about work, housing, and relationships. To her credit, she developed strong opinions on each and a keen desire for independence. I knew I needed to learn a lot from Gwen and her determination to stand tall and chart her own course every day.

At 16, Madolyn came down the stairs one evening hesitantly asking Jennifer and me, "Can we talk?" She sat down on the couch between us and began to share, "I've thought a lot about things, who I am, what I'm about, who I like, and, well, I'm gay." Jennifer and I had always taken pride in the level of communication and sharing we had with each of the kids. It was quite different from the reserved atmosphere we both grew up in.

Yet Madolyn's pronouncement was quite a shock. We hadn't had any such conversation on the subject leading up to that moment. She hadn't been on many dates and hadn't talked much about boys, but I was a shy, late-bloomer as well. We listened and heard a level of confidence and relief in her voice. She had clearly been thinking a lot about it and had come to realize her own comfort level. We shared our love for her bravery and asked how we might support. "Just being there for me is enough," she cried. I thought her revelation was so courageous. It surely would introduce personal struggles, bullying, and public recrimination. No doubt, it would not be easy. Yet she was ready to manage these stresses with a sense of honesty, humility, and humor that made us proud. I wish I'd been as brave during my hardships.

When Noah was about 12, I gave him my copy of *Quiet* by Susan Cain—basically the bible for introverts. I learned so much about myself and the world around me from that book. I thought Noah might appreciate the book during his adolescent development. He rejected the book, however, not just because of his pre-teen disdain for reading, but more so to dispute my diagnosis. In the years since, Noah has proven to be quite a socialite, amassing a quality group of friends at school and becoming a leader, not only in his school but also at his international HaZamir Jewish choir. He seemed to approach each situation toward developing a relationship, getting to know people. His high school yearbook was filled with terms of endearment from students and teachers alike. He may still be somewhat introverted. Like most of us, he still gets nervous in new situations. Yet he doesn't let that define or limit him. And I've learned not to do that to him, either. He manages to relax, share, and bond with people most everywhere. I can certainly benefit from his engaging manner to help me build relationships in the workplace and at social outings.

Jennifer has first and foremost been a mom. She opted not to return to work after Gwen was born to help nurture each of the kids. She set a high bar for herself, questioning any time she used fostering other talents. Though her creativity bloomed through scrapbooking, photography, and painting, family always came first. She not only captured vacations through pictures, but everyday events as well. Her intent was not just to preserve the memories we later huddled to re-share, but also to create the moments themselves, hand in hand, hugging, making funny faces together. Jennifer was constantly the one to gather us around the table for dinners and to ensure not only holidays but most weekend activities were family events. Now that the kids were older, the proof of her love and devotion was evident through our strong family bond.

Amazingly, when I finally lifted my head up after months grieving the loss of my father, my hero, I realized I was surrounded by other heroes showing me the way. Gwen's swagger, Madolyn's courage, Noah's social skills, and Jennifer's focus on family were just the characteristics I'd been searching for in my life. The perfect role models were right in front of me.

SECTION SIX – COURAGE

CHAPTER 27: SHIT!

After making considerable progress toward my health and family goals in the four years since our return from London, my bike accident had changed everything. However, by December 2013 my shoulder had achieved nearly full recovery after six months of intense rehab. Nevertheless, the bones were not the only things I shattered that day.

I had dropped 20 pounds while I awaited surgery and physical therapy due to muscle loss from a lack of movement and a diminished appetite. I was nearly 170 pounds for the first time in decades. My face looked sunken and my clothes slid off me. I received compliments from everyone, but I knew this was not really because of any great effort on my part.

As my appetite returned, the weight started to come back with a vengeance that fall. Feeling overwhelmed by the rehab, my return to work, and Dad's passing, I couldn't muster any self-control around my eating. Despite efforts to curb my intake, each attempt was futile. The word "failure" constantly rang in my head. My weight soared from 170 pounds to 200, 220, 240. Within six months after the accident, my "optimal" body had deteriorated, and my confidence was shot. SHIT!

After a couple of years in midstream my manager, Marcus, had taken the opportunity for early retirement. The management style of his replacement, Dave Trussel, was to support staff and rely upon them to run the organization. This fit well with my independent approach, but as 2013 drew toward a close, I was ready to move on. I had met my objectives of sustainable change in a rapidly evolving business. After five years in the job, I was in jeopardy of losing my energy, of perhaps being pigeonholed as a midstream specialist instead of the supply chain generalist I'd always been. With Dave's support, I began to evaluate other Shell jobs. In October, I identified a perfect role as Supply Manager for our Motiva joint venture. Not only would the role lean on my scheduling and trading pedigree, but also I would be working for Paul Douglas, a mentor from my earliest days at Shell and a very laid-back, personable leader. As the evaluation process continued, I had an interview with Paul that felt more like a coffee chat. During the hour we casually talked about expectations, challenges, and style. My experience was a natural fit and I expected an offer that I was prepared to enthusiastically accept in the coming weeks.

Meanwhile, as fate would have it, Shell was once again preparing to downsize. An energy industry downturn resulting from slumping oil and gas prices hit especially hard. The company announced a series of budget cuts and a reorganization of many senior management roles. New leadership brought a sense of urgency and increased focus on financial performance. However, this wave of new leaders immediately discounted the experience and relationships existing staff had cultivated and appeared to lay blame at the feet of current managers. For midstream, Dave was escorted out of Shell and the gas and crude oil midstream groups were now to be combined.

The new midstream manager, Carolyn Regan, arrived from Shell in New Orleans to carry the banner of change. Things were happening quickly. All staff wondered if they still had a job and, if so, what role they might play. I felt safe in the fact that the Motiva Supply Manager's job was likely to extract me from this chaos, though I was concerned about the destruction within my team that might be left in the wake.

Just as I awaited word from Motiva, Carolyn arranged our first meeting over breakfast. She explained her determination to introduce consolidation and change. I shared that I was seeking a new challenge and was posting on another role. She asked if I would consider joining her team to lead the transformation. I always had a passion for implementing organizational change and have remained a loyalist to my staff, especially through tough times. Perhaps this was an opportunity to lead my team through this change rather than run, as I had done when leaving fuel oil for London nearly a decade earlier. So, after our brief breakfast and some soul searching, I accepted Carolyn's offer and with much remorse, pulled my name from consideration for Paul's Supply Manager role.

I was rejuvenated by the idea of working to combine our gas and oil midstream teams and to realize the efficiencies that lay under the surface. However, after accepting Carolyn's invitation, I quickly found our styles were less than compatible. I was a trusting and loyal individual, sometimes to a fault, while she was skeptical and controlling. I craved and needed small but occasional recognition; however, she was just not that kind of person.

It became obvious the thrust from the very top was that managers must know the details of their business in order to drive the financially focused change that the shareholders demanded. Carolyn's interpretation of this new mindset was that her managers should personally know the minutest level of every aspect. This was in stark contrast to my team-based leadership style. Heck, Shell itself had drained that focus out of me years ago when I moved into my first supervisory job. They encouraged me to leave the specifics to my staff and concentrate on the bigger picture. Now Carolyn was, in essence, asking me to abandon my approach and do both: be the detail expert and the team leader.

Carolyn began interrogating her direct reports on every element of their business. She didn't like my style of referencing staff and their deep expertise. I realized her approach represented the changes throughout Shell. She was just doing her job in the style she knew best. But that didn't quell my rising frustration.

At Carolyn's February 2014 leadership meeting, she emphasized one of her core principles: that she neither recognized nor credited past accomplishments or loyalty, but that staff must earn that trust going forward. Until that point, she would double check and monitor the details for each of us. This struck right at my heart, disregarding my principles of trust and teamwork. Try as I might, I could not overcome this clash and it began to infect my whole self, so much that the stench of exasperation wafted outward to Carolyn, to my team, and to my home life.

Within a couple of months, Carolyn and I were having candid discussions during which she listed my apparent shortcomings and urged me to "get with the program." I could not, yet I was unable to articulate my position adequately. I felt like I was cowering in the corner, taking my lashings. I had come so far since arriving in midstream, yet when I was truly tested I became that six-year-old once again, stuffed in a closet waiting for someone to open the door.

By May, Carolyn and I both knew this experiment was not going to work. Six months after foregoing a dream job, I was now told to find another one. I couldn't stay in this role. I was not financially able to retire. I couldn't return to trading after the London debacle. And with Shell downsizing, shifting businesses within middle management could prove a tall order. SHIT!

I was literally shaking in my chair in her corner office, not just from the concerns of providing for my family, but also from my loss of confidence that seemed to erase all the progress I'd made since 2008.

As always, Jennifer stood by my side. She understood my dilemma and encouraged my job search. Yet she could see the worry on my face, and my expanding waistline.

As Carolyn looked to replace me, humiliated and disgraced, I moved to a "special project" until I found my next role, or until Carolyn tired of carrying my financial burden on her group's budget and decided to release me from Shell. I was just a blink of an eye from the stage of confidence and low stress I had proudly attained just a year earlier, before my bike accident, before Carolyn. I fell to another low point, reminiscent of the winter of 2008 in London, but this was worse. All my hard work since then seemed wasted.

As summer ended, I felt compelled to join Shabbat services on the one-year anniversary of Dad's passing. I stood listening to the service but, overwhelmed by emotions, I was unable to pay attention. I was deep in reflection. *I don't think I've made him proud this past year. I have wallowed about my shoulder injury instead of putting it behind me. I've been steamrolled by my boss, unable to champion my convictions. I have spent the last several months very bitter and lacking confidence rather than searching for my next job opportunity.*

Dad may have struggled through financial crises and many unwanted job changes, but he tackled each with dignity and honor. I had not really lived up to his example in my interactions with Carolyn or in the aftermath. It was time to make him proud. Enough wallowing or hating. It was up to me to change my attitude and turn the page on this chapter.

Thus, I recommitted myself to moving forward in search of a brighter future. With 26 years at Shell, this process was an exhaustive stretch for me. Equipped with lessons from my London transition six years earlier, I collected myself. Shell was a big company, so finding a commercial, supply chain role would take diligence to uncover the nooks and crannies. My reserved nature made this process frustrating and stressful, but my compulsive behavior drove me through it. I needed to move on, and return to the more confident, healthy, family man I had achieved just a year earlier. I created a spreadsheet and a plan of attack.

Finally, in December, I found a unique role, Supply Manager for Shell's bitumen business (largely the liquid component of road asphalt). I had several interviews with the posting manager, Angra Mainyu, who sought to assure himself that Carolyn's concerns had all been addressed and were non-issues. The role appeared to be a combination of the supply coordination Paul's Motiva posting had offered and the fuel oil trading role I had treasured 10 years earlier. The job, the vision, the familiarity, the limited travel, but broad end-to-end scope of the role was all very attractive. The group had been struggling to manage operational and commercial risks, which had cost the business millions in 2014. They were in desperate need of supply chain expertise to manage the increasing complexity. I was the perfect candidate. Finally, in the early days of 2015, Angra offered me the role of Supply Manager for Shell's bitumen business.

The demeaning struggles of the last year were over. I had finally landed a Supply Manager role that seemed to be my destiny all along. I was returning to the world of logistics, supply negotiations, and daily operational challenges that had energized me for the first half of my career. It was time to pick up the pieces of my shattered self. I coached myself to reassert my new leadership style and the personal confidence I had worked so hard to develop in midstream. I was ready to relax, flourish, and contribute, and Angra welcomed me to the team. Or so I thought…

On January 17, after accepting the role but before my official start date of February 1, I joined Angra for his full team meeting at a nearby hotel. It was a great opportunity to meet the team and hear their key priorities and issues for 2015. Unfortunately, what I discovered was the insulting temperament and communication style of its leader. Angra didn't just directly challenge his leaders and their staff in front of the full team, but he vilified them. He stood tall in his short frame, snaking around the room, pointing at various people, addressing them through his raised Indian accent.

"Why haven't you gotten this done earlier? I think you've done a bad job. What were you thinking?"

He denigrated not just one or two but the majority of the 25 people in attendance. As I peered around the room, I saw people afraid to make eye contact with Angra or even each other. This was a group broken down, living in fear. SHIT!

Perhaps performance was not up to standards, but Angra's approach was not helping the team make progress. By the end of the meeting, I could only ask myself, "What have I done?" Would this be another demeaning, destructive chapter for me?

Yet I related to the business and to the struggles of an oppressed team. I'd been there. Maybe I was in the right place. Maybe this was exactly where I was supposed to be.

In the coming weeks I met everyone on the bitumen team, including the five in my supply group. I could sense a passion for the relatively new business and personal dedication to help reverse the poor financial results. I was stimulated by the business and was thrilled to be involved in more commercial negotiations and small team leadership. Despite the bewildering management dynamics, we were making swift progress fixing past gaps and improving our cost of supply.

But I could also sense the tension that pervaded that conference room in mid-January. It all centered on Angra and his management style. One day he would yell at staff from across the floor, calling impromptu meetings to disparage their work and then abruptly changing focus to a new critical project or strategy. The next day he wanted to candidly discuss his shortcomings with me and genuinely asked for feedback, only to be followed by another shouting match that brought some staff to tears the next day. I became convinced this was not just an eccentric leadership style, but manipulative and abusive. It showed signs of someone who had a few screws loose.

Initially I just froze from disbelief. I provided little feedback to Angra and watched as he tore up staff, including a member of my supply team in a meeting. "You are incompetent! You are ill-prepared and can't answer my questions," he shouted.

Finally, my team member had been pushed past the brink and her courage burst into the room: "Enough! You have gone too far! I work so hard for this team. I'm up late and I try my best. You are rude and mean! I can't take it anymore! I am going to HR!" She stormed out of the room in streaming tears.

"She worked until late in the night preparing for this meeting, Angra," I retorted later. "Honestly, it's hard to anticipate the questions you will ask or the purpose behind some of the tasks you give her." My defense of her was met with harsh rebuke. He was in no mood to be challenged. He insisted she not return to the job and ostracized her to another floor while she posted for a new role. It was so demeaning, even eclipsing my project roles in London and midstream after bearing the wrath of my own headstrong managers.

Angra insisted on everyone following his decisions. He reached a boiling point quickly and had little patience for challenge, unless he himself invited it. I had to fall in line or become a target myself. Now I was being asked to change into someone I was not. Perhaps as a young professional I would have just accepted the direction and adjusted accordingly.

However, I had faked it for so long. I saw how destructive such a mismatch had been for me. I had come too far in the past few years to revert to my old style.

I had developed a humble yet firm level of bravado earlier in midstream. Inspired by my strong family, I had grown since my debacle with Carolyn a year earlier. My conviction to stand tall was rekindled. I couldn't tolerate another belittling job. It was time to punch my way out of that closet once and for all.

One afternoon Angra invited me in for discussions, which rapidly deteriorated into a tirade. "I need to be in your meetings with customers. I want to know about all your phone calls," he squawked.

I managed to keep calm and professionally defended myself and diffused his rant. "Angra, with all due respect, that doesn't make sense. We are aligned on strategic direction. Why do you insist on micromanaging? The team needs you at a higher level. They can't really function with you in the room all the time. Let me do what you hired me for. Then you can judge our results." Our matches often ended with Angra's closing outburst and a threat to my job. Though drained, I left the meetings with my head held high, acknowledging the heartfelt glances received from staff along the way back to my desk. As wrenching as these debates were, I was proud to stand my ground and defend my honor and that of my hard-working team.

Meanwhile, Angra did a great job of preserving his empire. He ruled by fear within his team and yet he managed his leader, Lester, who resided in Singapore, artistically. Lester appeared convinced Angra was an exceptional leader. When Lester and his management team came to the States, Angra put on a most constructive and empathetic façade. He had them convinced of his success in leading a well-run, united team.

During those leadership visits that spring, Lester and his team had one-on-one meetings with the Houston leadership group as a means of introduction and to gauge the pulse of our team. I casually shared some of my observations and excitement regarding the state of our business in a very simple and non-abrasive way, opting not to expose the harshness of the situation. "I'm excited about the opportunities in the market. We are quite busy and sometimes struggle to prioritize the many tasks, but we are making progress. We'll get there."

However, Angra went ballistic. He felt any discussions with Lester could reveal a bit of the nasty underbelly that Angra himself had created. After Lester's departure, Angra worked quickly to secure alignment by fear, threat, and belittlement. He pointed directly at me, "Steve. What did you tell them? My authority depends on their confidence. Why are you undermining me? You made me look like a fool!"

My defense fell on deaf ears.

Before Lester's next visit a few months later, Angra was sure to frame all discussions and forewarn everyone, most especially myself, not to deviate from the script. His leadership team closed ranks to survive this scorn, but we all suffered, displaying our stress through rashes, weight gain, lack of sleep, and emotional torment.

Yet, I continued to conduct myself in a professional way. The supply team improved costs and simplified procedures. I sought to provide a barrier as much as possible and defend their efforts against his attacks. I was certainly exhausted from the constant battles, but proud to stand up to the challenge with my principles intact.

Finally, about nine months into my tenure, karma caught up with Angra Mainyu. At a farewell party for one of his staff the summer of 2015, someone claimed Angra overstepped his bounds with an individual. This prompted a complaint to be filed with human resources and a detailed investigation ensued. Reminiscent of the fuel oil ethics case of 10 years earlier, the investigation appeared to be unable to prove the harshest of these claims. However, Pandora's box was opened and, through interviews with most staff, Shell discovered the harassing leadership style that everyone had endured. During the two-month investigation, Angra reached out to staff, trying to identify the collaborators and to shame people into silence. Yet the seeds were sown and by mid-autumn it became clear a leadership change was ahead.

SHIT! It was over and I was proud of how I'd handled a most difficult situation. I'd weathered the storm and come out with my integrity intact.

Lester and his management group stepped in to provide counseling and support for our leadership team. Though they still appeared suspicious of the findings, given the exceptional stakeholder management skills which Angra had employed, they vowed to quickly introduce a more people-oriented manager for the bitumen team.

CHAPTER 28: BURSTING

By Thanksgiving announcements were made and Bob Gunter, a Shell lubricants and retail manager, was introduced as our new leader. Seemingly overnight the veil was lifted. Bob introduced himself. He recognized the sensitivity of the situation but did not dwell on the past. He got to know his new team and emphasized his priorities of people and culture, which were sure to unleash the financial potential of the business itself. Bob unofficially tapped me as his right-hand man and confidante, and I was thrilled. He truly cared and was happy to enlist the leaders in reforming the culture and strategy. Suddenly, no longer masked by Angra's reign, all the exciting reasons why I took this job in the first place came to the surface. The whole team's collective sigh of relief was felt across the work floor.

Reinvigorated by Bob's recognition and guidance, we continued to generate new supply opportunities and improvements. The financial results steadily improved over the next couple of years. The staff and I finally felt supported, respected, and aligned. My craving for trust and independence was finally quenched after being absent these last couple of years.

Work was challenging while exciting and rewarding as well. The first summer together, Bob called a strategy workshop for the full team. It was a great opportunity for everyone to brainstorm, evaluate, and prioritize initiatives that addressed existing bottlenecks to profitability with focus on customer needs.

I was finally back in a good place, for the first time since my early fuel oil days 15 years prior. But this time I was not leaning on alcohol to get me through the tougher spots. Instead I was using my own style and renewed confidence to make better decisions and tackle customer situations through a team approach, rather than isolated on an island. Here, too, we had industry conferences with large cocktail hours. Yet this time I joined the networking socials with supportive team members and left when my rounds were complete—sober and well before my anxiety kicked in. I focused my time on structured small group meetings with key customers and suppliers, thus engaging with them in more comfortable settings.

Reassured by my renewed style and the supportive working culture, my stress level declined considerably. I was able to spend more quality time with the family and refocus on my health as my bike accident slid into the distance. Now, finally relaxed and happy, I began in earnest to tackle my 80-pound weight gain since my shoulder surgery.

Guided by doctors to forgo biking for other exercise that was slower and closer to the ground, I rediscovered my personal challenge in running. In February 2015 I literally pulled my 250-pound frame off the couch and began an alternating one-minute run/walk regimen on the treadmill. Eventually, my determination helped me complete over a dozen 5Ks in the spring and summer. I felt proud of my fast progress and accomplishments.

As with biking before, I was neither the fastest nor the slowest, yet I was content to run against my own goals—though a spirited kick at the end never hurt. I did collect a third place ribbon in my age group for one run, though I had to sprint past a few men with walkers to secure the prize. Excited by my progress and swept away by my addictive need for more, I soon enrolled in the Houston Half Marathon.

I was again in pursuit of another extreme goal for myself. I geared up, scheduling training runs up to 14 miles on the road and in the gym.

Finally, I made my way to the starting line with thousands of others on a warm, muggy day in January 2016. I ran my race and finished in just under three hours, limping across the finish line as my right leg cramped up in my effort to sprint the final couple of blocks. Proud, smiling, and exhausted to the point of sleeping on my recovery meal, I had completed another personal stretch goal.

However, as I reflected on my accomplishment and next steps, I realized my extreme adventures were not necessary. The constant pushing for more was both physically and mentally draining and had proven unsustainable time and time again. Thus, I opted for variety through brisk workouts in the gym and occasional 5K jogs in the neighborhood. I didn't need to prove anything to my family or myself. I was finally at peace with my exercise program.

No longer compelled to reside outside my comfort zone, I found a better balance in my life. I spoke up with confidence at our team meetings. I got more involved in career development and mentoring discussions, both with my staff and other younger employees. Better understanding myself, I often enjoyed the solitude of lunch alone on campus to recover from my daily social exertion. This provided me with time to revitalize and reflect. I shared my work satisfaction and energy with the family, now without any need to be ashamed or hide portions of my work life. We spent more time together and any tension in the house seemed to evaporate. Given the new environment Bob ushered in at work and the personal growth I'd found at home, I was on a path of healing which was both satisfying and long overdue.

Jennifer, my steadfast champion through the toughest of times, was not just my wife and partner but my everything.

She not only provided the warmth I craved in my early twenties but also the unwavering support as I struggled with alcohol, difficult work bosses, and my own self-esteem issues. Jennifer had the courage to steer me back onto the right path when I needed it most, all the while nurturing an incredible trio of children. Though my kids were not aware of most of my struggles with self-confidence or my disastrous attempts to cope with my introverted personality amidst the challenges of corporate ladder-climbing, they were my beacon through the toughest of times.

Meanwhile, Bob's leadership spawned many initiatives that continued to build the business, improving efficiency, reducing cost, and evolving team culture. But while the business's financial performance progressed year after year, we still fell short of our targets. Five years since startup, our senior leadership's patience and commitment were wearing thin. As the industry continued to tighten its belt, Shell re-focused its strategy on core businesses that promised stronger financial performance.

Hence, much of bitumen's 2017 was dedicated to a strategic review. I was part of a select group charged with evaluating the entire business, trying to find a path to greater profitability. Unfortunately, by the fall the team concluded that key parameters of our business presented systemic barriers to success. Suddenly, business closure became the obvious solution. Though the process was thorough, I was saddened by the conclusion. This business, and especially this team, had reinvigorated me. In just three years the people shrugged off the suppressing culture of Angra and created a stronger business and a tight-knit team. Yet despite best efforts, we had fallen short of our goals.

And thus another change was coming for me. As I recognized in the waning days of our fuel oil trading team 13 years earlier, all good things must come to an end. The end of

2017 presented each team member with the option of posting for another job in Shell or taking a package to retire or leave Shell for other opportunities.

In the past, when these types of critical junctures presented themselves, the decision may have been obvious but the courage to make the right choice and follow through with the tough actions necessary were not so easy. With my alcohol dependency and DUIs, as well as my stressful work situations in London and midstream, I needed others to push me to action.

This decision was also difficult. In good times and bad, work was what I had known. It consumed my focus and energy. I had imagined that retirement was still several years off, around age 55, so the prospect of this time frame caught me off guard initially. I tempered my instinct to grab the opportunity. I needed to ensure retirement would be prudent and feasible. I did not want to forgo our dreams of travel and hobbies. Nor did I want to have to return to work to ensure our nest egg would last.

Hence, I conducted my own due diligence. I contacted my financial advisor who reviewed our position and desired lifestyle and deemed retirement feasible. I contemplated retired life and feverishly started a list of interests, hobbies, and travels to ponder how I might spend my time. Jennifer and I discussed such a radical lifestyle change for us, and we both became thrilled.

I dismissed co-worker challenges that, at 52, I was too young to retire, as well as the naysayers who thought I was being forced out or had lost my edge. To the contrary, this was the opportunity to leave at the top of my game. I had finally embraced who I truly was and enjoyed the good fortune that surrounded me. Over the past 10 years I realized the ultimate prize for long term employees at Shell was reaching 30 years, at which point full medical benefits and pension would be provided. With my 30 years just months away, this benchmark was finally possible.

I received Bob's assurance I could stay to my anniversary in June, and then I opted for retirement. This time, with the support of Jennifer and the family, I had made the difficult and right choice. Each day after my decision, I got more enthusiastic about the impending change until I nearly burst during my commutes home. Jennifer was equally ecstatic about the opportunity for us to spend more time together. She remarked that she could see the tension flow out of me. "I haven't seen you so relaxed in years!" Many, many years.

During the first six months of 2018, as people posted to other Shell jobs or moved on for work elsewhere, I supported them with mentoring and counseling while negotiating many of our remaining business obligations with external counterparts. How fitting that I was asked to stay to provide my commercial and engagement skills toward the business closure, those tasks which caused me most stress and grief throughout my career. I did my best before shifting focus in the final weeks to the more reserved and menial tasks necessary to close the doors. Throughout this period, I began transitioning mentally from the work world which I had often loved and occasionally just survived to what I hoped would be an extension of the healthier and happier family life I'd been dreaming of the last six months.

On June 9, 2018, I celebrated my month-end retirement from Shell, just three days after achieving my long-sought 30 years of service. Family and friends from across the years joined my retirement party to toast a long career. Many toasters recalled my early, shy days just learning the landscape, others the intense leadership training at Detroit in the mid-90s. Still others shared the team camaraderie and alcohol-laden experiences within fuel oil across the millennium, and finally more recent teammates recalled my mentoring and supply initiatives with midstream and bitumen.

It was strange to have so many people from across the years and roles in one room. As each speaker shared unique, funny, successful, and cloudy moments, I observed others in the audience laughing, nodding their head in recollection, and a good portion silent, with their eyebrows curled up in confusion. This was not the Steve Friedman they had experienced. The co-workers in midstream and bitumen couldn't place me as the party guy of my fuel oil and LPG trading days. The folks that welcomed me into Shell in the late '80s hadn't envisioned the commercial leader I would become three decades later. So many recognized the person from their era, but not where I began or who I had become.

Jennifer stood by my side during the toasts as she had for nearly 30 years, cheering me on, supporting me, and guiding me. All three kids joined in celebrating my career just as I reveled in their successes. I realized none of the attendees except for my family truly knew the real me. I had put on a series of facades for three decades. Business books and leadership seminars would half-jokingly use the phrase "fake it 'til you make it," and I had done just that. Not by choice, but by necessity.

As a timid and reserved person, I had somewhat mocked other retirees over the years who maintained that it was the people that made the difference in their career and what they would remember most. Despite many business and relationship successes, working with others contributed to the draining of my energy. I had stepped out of my comfort zone daily, to put on a more sociable face to all these people. I'm not sure I fooled anyone. When Bob bought me a shirt that read, "I have CDO, It's like OCD but all the letters are in alphabetical order as they should be," I blushed at this truth, and realized perhaps my façade was a bit more transparent than I'd expected. I was never the most sociable, outgoing, flamboyant, or engaging personality in the room, but in my own way I pushed myself to lead. I knew I was better for it and hoped those I worked with might say the same. I shared my sentiments in the final lines of my toast to staff:

I'm really not the most social, outgoing sorta guy,
So it kinda surprises me to say this with a tear in my eye…

But amongst all the businesses and stories to tell,
None would be the same without you, the great people
of Shell.

I also toast my lovely bride and three magnificent children,
Who lived through my travels and stress since way back
when.

I have lots of cool plans with my family from this day on,
So, raise your glasses, thank you all, may we all ROCK ON!

In reality, I believe I related to everyone in that room in different ways. Some I mentored, others I toiled alongside, a few I drank with to escape or celebrate, and still others perhaps I frustrated. Yet, the laughs, struggles, and successes of the individuals and the teams we comprised formed the memories and legacy I left behind. With so many moments flashing through my mind that evening, I truly could say the people *did* make the difference. They drove me to be the best I could be, to learn, to work hard, to engage when I didn't want to engage, and to survive my struggles and realize my strengths.

CHAPTER 29: REFLECTIONS

During my final few weeks at Shell, I reflected on some of those who didn't attend my retirement party. In fact, amongst the hundred-plus invited, their names were intentionally left off. I recognized those I cursed over the years for what I viewed was malicious and destructive behavior and those for whom I was the damaging force. As such, I chose to reach out to these villains and victims, possibly to confront them, maybe to apologize, but certainly to learn and let go.

I had blamed people like Kenneth Braman in fuel oil, Harold Rudman and Nigel Foster in LPG, and Carolyn Regan in midstream for destroying productive work teams and creating extreme hardships in my life. But over time I realized no situation could be placed solely at the foot of one person. Some circumstances likely evolved from my own selfish approach to leadership or my own unhealthy habits during those periods. But, rest assured, most were created or exacerbated by poor communication all around.

When I reached out, I was nervous about the responses I might receive, yet pleased that I was finally able to rise above the conflicts and pursue a mature path toward healing. Most people did not respond to my invitation, perhaps understandably not interested in rehashing old issues that never took such a toll on them as they had on me. However, I did have a very pleasant lunch with Carolyn. We both acknowledged that the tension during our stretch together in midstream was unfortunate. I shared my pain and insecurity during that time. I offered my supposition that digging my heels in rather than trying to work out differences contributed to the malice. She shared her frustration with my lack of attention to detail that, in her view, approached insubordination. She was confused as to why I had pushed back, especially since she viewed me as the most experienced leader in her crusade for change. We lamented that such recognition had never been shared. Maybe we missed out on a bonding moment that could have made all the difference. Neither of us had communicated our needs or motivations. As a result, our divide grew. Perhaps it never would have worked out given our different styles, but we left our lunch more appreciative of each other's approach and prepared to apply our reflections toward those we love and lead going forward.

I also considered those I hurt, especially my childhood best friend Roger Bates. I had disassociated myself with him during middle school, even resorting to petty name-calling to try to impress other kids. After four decades, Roger and I were able to reconnect. We struck up a conversation over Facebook Messenger, during which I apologized for my immature behavior in middle school. He didn't recall the specifics but suggested we just grew apart and he carried no ill will. I felt such relief for a burden I had carried for so long. We used to play with matchbox cars in the dirt of his backyard and jump our bikes over homemade ramps. Roger has since become a motorcycle repair shop owner and cross-country racer. I'm so proud of him for pursuing a dream that perhaps hatched during our time together.

My conversations with Carolyn and Roger, along with my efforts to contact others, helped settle my gnawing guilt.

Sometimes it amazed me to have survived and generally thrived at Shell in jobs that were exciting yet exhausting, bringing me to the brink of upper management and to the edge of personal disaster. Some may wonder if I hold any ill will toward my long-term employer. I never blamed Shell for my struggles. In fact, Shell often exceeded my expectations in the way they treated employees; for example, they gave me time to find new roles and accommodated my two-month absence as I recovered from shoulder surgery. I also recognized I would not be in such a position to retire early and begin a new phase of my life if not for the benefits of Shell.

To the contrary, I usually blamed myself for my struggles. I faulted my own introversion, even before I fully understood what that was. Weak, I succumbed to the negative public perception of introversion. Without education and self-reflection, my own personality was both frustrating and degrading to me. I also recognized that my need to provide for my family drove me up the corporate ladder. But I didn't realize the price I'd pay for such determination until I was already engulfed in my own anxiety and my family got the scraps left over after long, arduous workdays.

During much of my life, my introversion and addictive nature had battled to establish a tenuous equilibrium. I coped with the stress at work resultant from my many social tasks by becoming a workaholic, social alcoholic, morbidly obese glutton, and whirlwind global traveler. Later, my compulsion to stretch myself to extreme goals led me to tackle 170-mile bike rides and a 13.1-mile half marathon. One avenue appeared healthier than the other, yet my inability to control such extremes was troubling in either case. But it was my way of trying to hide my stress and maintain some sort of teetering balance in my life. While my journey of extremes has been truly memorable and provided a bit of the spice of life, the ride also provided periods of intense stress, frayed relationships, and doctors' warnings.

In those last weeks at Shell, I sought to contemplate key forks in the road. I pondered what life would have been like if I had been more confident, more outgoing, more vibrant and engaging, and, well, more extroverted. Would I have had the same life? Would it have been better? Less stressful? More successful? If I were outgoing, what society might classify as more "normal," could I have achieved more at work? Could I have schmoozed a bit more with stakeholders, staff, and managers? Could I have advocated my point of view on projects more definitively and received more recognition and promotions? Could I have been more flexible or forceful in working with the challenging variety of managers I endured during the second half of my career? Could I have been more successful in my role in London and not succumbed to the disasters of my addictions?

Or perhaps I've been in the wrong career all along? What if I'd chosen writing instead of business those many years ago? Such a typically introspective profession could have provided a better fit for me—one suited to my personality, so I could thrive without the tremendous stress I had to endure. Rather than pick up writing in my 50s, perhaps I would have discovered this energy years ago.

So, would I have chosen a different personality or path if that were afforded to me?

To answer that question, I've had to take stock of my life these last few years. Over time, perhaps with maturity or possibly through the hard-fought scars collected, I've grown to appreciate the strengths and values of introverts—of myself—analytical, self-reflective, structured, thoughtful, creative, expressive. Now I'm no longer wracked with guilt and shame. I am striving to embrace my introversion and refine my personal talents.

As I ponder my college and career choice when I was in my teens, perhaps as my parents suspected, I would have joined many other creatives in the daily grind to put food on the table.

In that case, maybe I would have merely traded off the stress of social engagement for the pressure to provide for my family. That may have been just as hard to cope with for three decades.

Finally released from the bonds of Shell, I understand no one is really to blame for my hardships or my poor coping mechanisms. Like most people, I was just trying to figure out who I was and how to provide for my family. I now realize this path was neither as quick nor as simple as I would have liked, but it was a journey I had to take to reach this point of self-awareness and growth.

Ultimately, if life had plotted out a different path—whether extrovert or writer—I likely would not have met Jennifer at the bowling alley in 1990. I am nothing without her and my family. I can't imagine going through life—any life—without them. I'm surrounded by love and have earned the self-respect that has made me stronger and more excited about my future.

Finally, at the end of June, I officially retired from Shell. I'd been pinching myself for the last six months in anticipation of this day. Now it was here, and I beamed with astonishment as I closed the door to this chapter of my life. I had pulled it off! I turned in my laptop and cell phone. I picked up my box of knick-knacks. I said my goodbye to those still in the office, and I walked out of Shell for the last time with a big smile on my face!

For my retirement, Jennifer bought me a shirt: "Introverts Unite—We're Here, We're Uncomfortable, and We Want to Go Home." I was ready to go home.

So, no, I wouldn't trade my life for anyone's. I now have the courage to achieve both of my dad's goals—the warm family experience he championed and the impassioned creative living that only filled his dreams. Sounds like the perfect life to me!

EPILOGUE

June 9, 2019

I worked for just over thirty years. As I walked out of the Shell building a year ago, I admittedly was both excited and nervous. Work had occupied most of my waking hours. I had quality moments with Jennifer and the kids only in my spare time. Though I'd compiled a wish list of hobbies, I really didn't have the inclination to carve out the time for any while working. I was not a golfer, fisherman, woodworker, or socialite, that's for sure. Yet, I was excited to leap to this next phase of life. As satisfied as I was with my Shell career, I was convinced my new life would be stupendous. A year later, I can certainly say it's been all that and more.

After all these years, I had two key lessons to guide me.

First and foremost, I wanted to embrace my true self. I'm proud to be an introvert. Rather than absorb all my energy pushing myself out of my comfort zone in order to perform for others, I wanted to leverage that creativity, thoughtfulness, and introspection to contribute to my family and myself. I was convinced that harnessing these neglected strengths would bring relaxation and happiness.

But I also had to wrestle with my innate desire to push myself to extremes. Whether alcohol, work, gambling, or exercise, this addictive behavior was part of my DNA, but it was called to the forefront too often to counterbalance the stresses at work. Such extremes had proven to be unhealthy throughout my past. I had to accept that those headline moments of drinking to unconsciousness or excessive exercising beyond the point of exhaustion were not necessary to live a fun and memorable life. And they weren't necessary to relieve the strain of social moments. I needed to recalibrate my definition of success from activities that punish me to those that bring joy to my life. I had to redefine my priorities and drive moderation into my life.

Motivated by these two beliefs, I reviewed my two-page catalog of interests compiled since the end of 2017. My long list was encouraging, but I was concerned I might overwhelm myself by tackling everything at once. I wanted to make a difference in my life and in that of my family. So, I concentrated on the priorities I had developed in the past couple of years: health, family, and writing. These have been my focus. This past year I defended my time to ensure I dedicated my hours to making a difference in these three areas.

My health had stabilized in the past couple of years but was far from ideal. I started to meet with a coach who guided me to focus on mindfulness and moderation. Rather than target a particular weight and adhere to a strict diet of numbers, I was encouraged to be mindful, to think about whether I was truly hungry before and during meals. I also needed to consider what I was really hungry for, what would satisfy me. If that was salad, or chicken, or a cookie, so be it. Without the constraints of calorie counting, the system seemed so easy. It was dependent on my being in touch with myself, actually using my introverted personality. The goal was merely to be satisfied: with my meals, with my looks, and with myself. It relieved the pressure I had put on myself.

If I find such satisfaction at 230 pounds or at 180 or elsewhere, that is fine. This mindset takes time—time to relax, gain awareness, and make conscious decisions. I'd never had that space while I was working. But now I prioritize my days. Now, mindfulness pervades my life, relaxing me and yet driving me toward fulfillment.

I was excited to restructure my fitness program. Without the convenience of the Shell gym, I joined a local facility. But instead of pushing myself to new heights or distances or speeds, my emphasis has been on moderation and control. My challenge is not to push myself to get off the couch and go to the gym. For me, that's easy. My test is to actually slow down, ratchet back a bit so that I'm not pushed to extremes that have inevitably resulted in harmful repercussions later. Instead of a strict schedule of activities, I literally walk into the gym and choose what I want to do that day: stationary bike, elliptical, weights, stairs, or treadmill. I've even joined Jennifer at Pilates Reformer and yoga, both of which I find to be exceptional workouts of the core and mind.

This has introduced a level of self-control and flexibility that, in my past, I had struggled to find. A year later, I've lost 40 pounds, but more notably my liver enzyme levels have consistently been normal for the first time since my teens and, most significantly, I'm happy and confident. This mindfulness and moderation program leverages my strengths to find peace.

Family time had been a rare commodity, enjoyed either as fleeting moments during weekends or often during frantic, highly scheduled family travels. Since retirement I'm taking a more leisurely yet impactful approach.

Gwen and I formalized her independence plan that focuses on the skills she needs to develop in order to live on her own within a few years. We believe, like her siblings, she can only go so far while staying within the comfortable and protective confines of our home. She needs and, most importantly, wants more independence in order to flourish. She is now waking to her own alarm, walking to her new job four days a week, doing her own laundry, learning about communications and relationships, and practicing other life skills. Her confidence is soaring and she is giddy in pursuit of her own dream of independence. When she succeeds with new tasks and hugs me while sporting her beaming smile, I couldn't be more satisfied.

While I was recovering from my bike accident, Madolyn toured colleges to further her dream as a stage manager in the theatre industry. She built on her position at the local Jewish Community Center and by the fall of 2014 Madolyn was off to Emerson College in Boston where she excelled on her own. She completed the rigorous schedule of courses and rehearsals at the top of her class.

After retirement, I helped her settle into her first apartment in New York City. A year later she has completed her one-year stage management fellowship off-Broadway, and we've thoroughly enjoyed visiting NYC for each of her three shows. It's amazingly gratifying and exciting to see how she combines her originality, passion, and kindness to present such a mature approach to life's challenges. This transition to a new life in New York has not always been easy. Yet as opposed to the dangerous coping mechanisms I reached for, Madolyn instead has leaned on a support system of family and friends to weather storms. She has adopted a healthy and active lifestyle and continues to build friends and networks in the Big Apple. I'm so proud of her choices and courage. Madolyn and I have a fun connection jogging in the city and talking about life and leadership. We are very much alike in our resiliency and determination while, thankfully, she shares the spirit, creativity, and warmth of her mother.

Mid-way through high school, Noah has flourished at Houston's High School for the Performing and Visual Arts. He is mastering his vocal talents and gaining confidence in singing many solo classics in front of audiences. He has also groomed his vocal and mentoring talents as a leader for the HaZamir international Jewish choir, performing at Lincoln Center in New York the last few years. I continue to be in awe of his talent and inspired by his exuberant and social personality.

Noah and I had a blast grabbing a weekend in Austin in October to Segway, scooter, and see a show. He is blossoming into an awesome young man with the trepidation and excitement of his college search just around the corner.

Retirement has enabled Jennifer and me to reconnect in so many fulfilling ways. We share the house most days as she explores her amazing artistic talents through collage, paint, and pencil, while I write nearby. One of the most gratifying additions to my life is helping Jennifer display, market, and sell her creations within the Houston community. She has such magnificent talent and a pure desire to share her inspiring creations with others. We take breaks for meals together, along with Pilates, yoga, and a soothing monthly massage. Now more than ever, we are a partnership. I can never fully repay her for being my guiding light for all these years, but I'm having fun trying!

Finally, rekindling my dream of writing has not only fulfilled the promise to Mom and Dad, but more so to myself. I wanted to explore my past, my personality, and my life. It's been an exciting journey of writing, editing, and publishing that has leveraged my strengths and confirmed my ambitions. I've found the process to be therapeutic and nourishing, helping me to better understand myself as I am trying to become my best self.

Suddenly, I no longer seek to endure weekdays for two-day weekend reprieves. Now, I need the clock to slow down, so I can tackle the many stimulating aspects of my life today. Our Pilates teacher, who saw me struggle with the unexpectedly exhausting drills last year, recently remarked, "People hate what they can't do and stop. I place a challenge in front of you and you have never hesitated to meet it head on. You could have quit. Winners never quit. That's the tenacious spirit that equals to success that I admire. Your fortitude is amazing." What touching words that capture much of my approach during my life.

Over the past year as I chronicled my personal stories not only did I find the courage to embrace my introversion and control my addictions, but I also discovered that the only acceptance I truly need is from myself and my family. With that comfort, I look forward.

ACKNOWLEDGMENTS

When I started writing *In Search of Courage*, I could not have imagined the cast of people required to produce the final product. But over the past couple of years, I've had the very good fortune to find so many giving and talented people. I may have completed my project, regardless, but I'm sure the journey would not have been as rich, and the final product surely would not have been as compelling, if not for my support team.

Roger Leslie and I met at a local writer's conference. I found him engaging, wise, and kind through our lunchtime discussions. Six months later I asked him to coach me through the writing process and provide content editing throughout my project. A year later, he has been instrumental, not just in the final product, but in the depth of my personal learning throughout. Through his wisdom I continue to bare my soul and live unabashedly. Thanks, Roger. You're the best!

Paradise Publishing LLC, Roger Leslie, PhD, RogerLeslie.com

Laura Roberts, my copy editor, has done a marvelous job pulling all my sentences together in a coherent and proper manner. Thanks a ton, Laura.

Laura Roberts, LauraRobertsCreativeServices.com

Cathi Stevenson and **Gwen Gades**, the dynamic design duo, exceeded my lofty expectations. Cathi's cover and Gwen's formatting have made my book inviting and aligned with the vision and tone of my story. Your flexibility and communication were tremendous.

Book Cover Express, BookCoverExpress.com, Cathi Stevenson
Be a Purple Penguin, BeAPurplePenguin.com, Gwen Gades

A huge hug for my writing critique group ladies: Jean Nunnally, Margo Catts, Karen Hale, Amanda Olson, Ronarose Train. Each week you contributed your honest comments, challenges, ideas, and personal support. You are such a giving group and invaluable for both my writing and personal growth process this past year.

IN SEARCH OF COURAGE:
An Introvert's Story

I hope you have been captivated by my
experiences and inspired by my journey.

FREE BONUS – LOG IN FOR PHOTOS
FOR EACH CHAPTER

www.BeyondIntroversion.com/In-Search-of-Courage/Photos

Please join the journey on our website
and signup for the weekly blogs at:

www.BeyondIntroversion.com

Share your comments and questions with the author at:
BeyondIntroversion@gmail.com

Made in the USA
Monee, IL
09 August 2021